Clearings
in the Thicket

Clearings

in the Thicket:

An Alabama

Humanities Reader

Essays and Stories
from the 1983 Alabama History
and Heritage Festival

EDITED BY
JERRY ELIJAH BROWN

MERCER

ISBN 0-86554-144-2

All books published by Mercer University Press
are produced on acid-free paper that exceeds
the minimum standards set by the
National Historical Publications and Records Commission.

Library of Congress Cataloging in Publication Data

Alabama History and Heritage Festival (1983 :
Auburn, Ala.)
Clearings in the thicket.

Includes bibliographies.
1. Alabama—History—Congresses. 2. Alabama—
Fiction—Congresses. I. Brown, Jerry Elijah,
1945-   . II. Title.
F326.5.A43 1983   976.1   84-25589
ISBN 0-86554-144-2 (alk. paper)

Contents

"Alabama is named for the great river which drains its center. The river in turn received its name from the Ala-bamas, an early tribe of Indians which once lived on its banks at or near the present site of Montgomery. The name Alabama is of Choctaw origin and means 'thicket clearers.' . . ."

DEDICATION

To Robert Bennett Gilbert

He reads much,
He is a great observer, and he looks
Quite through the deeds of men.
     —William Shakespeare, *Julius Caesar, I, ii*

Acknowledgments

Several organizations and scores of Alabamians contributed directly and indirectly to this reflection of Alabama's humanities. The Committee for the Humanities in Alabama proposed the 1983 History and Heritage Festival, provided the basic grant, and worked with several universities, agencies, and private groups in coordinating the statewide celebration of Alabama life and letters. The Auburn University contingent benefited greatly from exchanges with other primary participants from the University of Alabama at Birmingham and Huntsville, the University of South Alabama, and the Montgomery Humanities Alliance, a consortium of several private and public agencies, and Auburn University at Montgomery. The John and Mary Franklin Foundation and its board chairman W. Kelly Mosley sponsored the visits of Lee Smith and James Haskins to the state conference in Auburn. The Alabama Cooperative Extension Service used its network to identify citizens across the state who were interested in the humanities and were eager to attend the conference. Auburn University's School of Arts and Sciences, led by Dean Edward H. Hobbs, and the Department of Continuing Education, directed by Dean Gene A. Bramlett, were the on-campus pillars for their institution's effort. This volume is published in part through a grant from The Humanities Fund of Auburn University.

Many organizations in Lee, Marengo, Barbour, and Calhoun counties lent their influence to the planning and publicizing of meetings. The success of Auburn's effort is in large measure the result of the leadership of Nancy and Forrest Shivers and John Fletcher of Opelika, Gwyn Turner of Demopolis, Marthur Houston and Douglas Clare Purcell of Eufaula, and Grace Gates of Anniston. Each of these local chairmen led a train of local citizens whose contributions fulfilled the aim of the festival. The scholars most directly involved in guiding the Auburn University humanities troupe across the state have essays in this volume. The amount of work they and many others did, in addition to their regular teaching and administrative duties, is a testament to their regard for the humanities and their attachment to Alabama's people. The essayists and storytellers gave their writings for use in this collection, and the individuals or publications holding rights to previously published works allowed their use without charge. A special note of gratitude is given to Bryan Easley and Jerry Medley for photography and graphics. Elsie Reynolds has been the exemplary typist and proofreader, from preface to index, and she deserves credit as serving as editor. This statement of acknowledgment to all others who contributed to this volume should be regarded as more than a mere formality.

An Editor's Preface:

Alabama's Humanities

JERRY E. BROWN

Words are the beacons of our humanity. They shine through the generations, brightening our imaginations and illuminating the values that make us a distinct, civilized people. In fact, we can call ourselves Alabamians, joining our personal identities with a human-wrought geographical unit, because a legacy of spoken and written language, of songs and memories brings this place to life. Times, events, and people have been observed, talked about, written about, and related to Alabama for over two hundred years of English-speaking society. Our claim to a culture is inseparable from the humanities—those works which use words to convey life's meanings—and yet paradoxically many of us do not know what the term means, nor do we grasp the breadth and strength of the humanities in Alabama. To realize that the humanities are vital, but that we seldom recognize the relationship between the humanities and humanity, is to see two pointed questions in need of answering: What is currently happening in Alabama to demonstrate the vitality of the humanities? And, more particularly, how can our everyday lives be improved by a fresh display of writings with a distinctive Alabama stamp?

This collection of works from Alabama attempts to address these fundamental questions. The responses, I hope, will not prove to be the textbookish kind that wither on the page. To be sure, the answers will not be at all direct; rather they will be living examples of how human experience takes on meaning as it takes on form—in this case, the forms of writing common to the humanities. Illustrated within this limited gathering are the personal essay, the short story, the scholarly article, the community chronicle, and the humorous sketch, several of which naturally overlap. The humanities find other expressions as well, among them the novel, the poem, the biography, and the film, in addition to several academic branches of study devoted to language, philosophy, anthropology, and archaeology. Any work not labeled as fine arts, science, or social science might be classified as humanities, but the term dies when it is used merely as a cataloguing device.

I still prefer to link the humanities to an older phrase, "the liberal arts," the meaning of which is almost lost these days. That term has at its root the concept of freedom. In reading and thinking about human experience, its variety of forms and meanings, we can liberate ourselves from the thickets of ignorance and isolation; we can free ourselves to join the company of all mankind; we can unite our knowledge and insight. I hope each work in this collection will confirm that definition of the humanities and, too, I hope that the definition will grow as the reader's experience touches the writer's. Each essay and story will, in its own way, imply that basic inquiry underpinning the humanities: *What does it mean to be human?* Works that stem from this universal question provide knowledge and entertainment and are likely to take on new meaning when they are discovered in a setting that is particular and familiar, this common ground—Alabama.

Brought together and published as a book for a wide audience of general readers, these writings form a body of evidence illustrating the value and persistence of the humanities. How this book came into existence is, in itself, one testament to the strength of the humanities in Alabama.

In 1983 the Committee for the Humanities in Alabama, a group of private citizens that distributes federal funds for worthy projects in history, literature, and other related pursuits, sponsored a state-wide festival to call attention to the significant explorations of the meaning and quality of life in Alabama. Auburn University was one participant in this History and Heritage Festival. Professors from the School of Arts and Sciences, guided by Missy Kuykendall, an able administrator from the Department of Continuing Education, planned meetings in Auburn, Demopolis, Eufaula, and Anniston. The gatherings provided opportunities for local citizens and working scholars—terms not mutually exclusive, it was demonstrated—to explore specific topics related to local interests. (Auburn's model for these meetings was the result of two successful years with Lee County historical associations.) Auburn's contribution to the state festival included well-known writers with Alabama connections, among them Harper Lee, James Haskins, and Lee Smith, who joined with university and local scholars to consider, for instance, how familiar materials become prize-winning short stories, what it means to grow up black in the Black Belt, and what is to be gained from reading again the blood-curdling tales of early historian Albert Pickett.

In looking over the essays and stories, many of which were speeches, and seeking special contributions from some of the participants, those of us who had attended and enjoyed the festival meetings saw that we might present a fair display of the humanities in Alabama from several quarters, in several forms, by representatives of many groups. The writings were all high quality essays that expanded a wide variety of subject matter and intent. Rooted in time and place, concentrating on specific topics, the festival participants nevertheless touched a general, but unifying, tradition and produced writings that deserved a wider audience. Although not planned as part of the original festival, this collection consists of individual works, valuable and interesting, that demonstrate the range and vitality of a particular inheritance.

To signify the peculiar, this anthology is called *Clearings in the Thicket*, reflecting the literal translation of the word *Alabama*. As such, the title coincides both with a concrete image of the humanities and with a generalized depiction of the ancestors who gave us this tradition. Works of the humanities do represent human clearings, moments when minds and hearts catch up to experience and make something from it. If there is meaning in life, where will it be stated? And where but in these clearings can experiences be kept, for more watching and more study?

It is one of the ironies of our past that Alabama's firm foundation in the humanities was laid by forebears too busy to place much value on the printed word, other than the Bible. Many were unschooled. They worked in fields, kitchens, mines, mills, logging woods, small stores, and the occasional office, classroom, or pulpit. They endured plague and panic, living through conditions that might otherwise have reduced us to savagery, and still they were able to convey to us the manners and the morals that are the hallmarks of our humanity. They knew those special clearings in the thickets of their lives and understood their value—times for deliberation and creation, and for passing on a virtue that cannot be purchased. Although these ancestors might not have known that they were fostering the humanities—perhaps the experiences they contemplated were disastrous—they were nonetheless placing a high premium on those moments when understanding breaks through. They knew how to make histories, to preserve values, to discover comedy, and to give immortality to characters. They also knew how to set the imagination free. The climate cultivated by the early nineteenth-century settlers prevailed through wars and social upheavals, and it has influenced each writer in this collection. Modern writers, like their ancestors, value the clear vision of a story told truthfully, without sentimentality. They also know that stories provide a special social bonding.

I cannot deny that there is another side to our humanities tradition. Although the heritage is real enough, we are a long way from being secure in it. If we could safely presume that Alabama—or the country or the world, for that matter—would always have a society in which the humanities might be recognized as being vital to our welfare, there would be little justification for this volume. But even those of us born after World War II can see how much has changed. The oral tradition that introduced most Alabamians to the humanities—a literary legacy from the pioneers—is disappearing. Even radio, which could speak to the imagination in a special way, has given way to television, which most often only numbs the brain. Our landscapes have been altered, usually for the worst. A Southern literary renascence has come and gone. To be sure, those of us most closely involved in appreciating the humanities feel a certain anxiety. What if a generation were to arise that possessed none of the cultural characteristics of these ancestors I have mentioned? Such a new generation would be self-contained, non-social, non-talkative, apathetic, materialistic, and without memory. Such fearsome folks would be the antithesis of the Alabamians who gave us our humanities tradition. They would not look to the humanities for sustenance; they would not want to make the effort to ponder the significance of human experience; and they would not feel the freedom of the humanities.

This fear of an alien, iconoclastic generation is at least as ancient as the Greeks, and the anthology in your hands will not conclusively put it to rest. However, these writings should illustrate that the humanities tradition, at this moment, is alive and well. Far from being anxious that the humanities are dying, I know that the values and the forms are timeless. Seeing the humanities practiced by people under forty also prompts me to take a leap of logic and faith and to conclude that the bequest is permanently transmissible: it can be passed on to other generations—forever. The settings may change from firesides and front porches, the expressions may change if tall tales give way to futuristic fantasies, but the humanities are likely to generate interest and to be associated with Alabama as long as the state has boundaries.

Although the impact of these new writings is heady enough to cause some wild surmises, I will stop short of saying that the humanities are Alabama's richest treasure. However, I cannot think of any human pursuit more capable of producing works of beauty, permanence, and value. A tradition that gives us a chance not only to see ourselves in creation but to add to that creation is a cultural legacy worth examining and worth perpetuating. It is especially heartening to see this tradition at work close to home in a clearly visible confirmation of an enduring truth: great literature always begins locally, amidst the confusion of flesh and blood and place. Even the famous works enshrined in classrooms and libraries—the novels of Dostoyevsky and Flaubert, the poetry of Yeats, the histories of Shelby Foote—deal with ordinary people in local settings. Unlike the works of science, these writings rarely aim for solutions; instead, they again prove the presence of those universal truths of our human nature. Works that begin as intensely local, even provincial, can rise above their particular worlds like full moons, gathering light from one limited source but reflecting it far beyond their own spheres.

The utility of this book will lie with the reader. For a more complete definition of the humanities, I suggest that readers pay close attention to the first title. It is written by three Auburn University scholars who represent the disciplines of history, English, and religious studies. Thereafter, new information may be gained about several Alabama writers, from early historians and travelers to such excellent but little-known writers as Lella Warren and Tom Sims. One may also see how historical, scholarly essays start as private questions but conclude as public presentations. One special, lasting pleasure should come as familiar characters take on full, comic lives in works of fiction.

Teachers and students, perhaps reading more closely than some, might notice that the Alabama experiences depicted in these writings tend to reflect the theme of survival-in-the-wilderness. This theme emerged subtly, without force; natural and social thickets were seen by the writers as factors in the strife encountered by future governors, lone preachers, religious communities, and forgotten books. The resulting struggles and the many triumphs produce that elevation of spirit that makes us praise individual works and recognize immediately the value of the humanities.

As a native Alabamian, I see this collection as both a sign and a promise. Alabama does contain a civilization that is as fragile and as enduring as life itself. The humanities are the arteries of that culture, bringing to it the nourishment necessary for survival; vessels that are this critical and life-sustaining need definition, recognition, and care. The coming together of a large number of citizens, many universities, and the Committee for the Humanities in Alabama is yet another sign that the humanities are considered more than ornament. Projects now underway across Alabama indicate that people are taking the time to ask questions about historical events, writers, and artists. Furthermore, the 1983 History and Heritage Festival and this collection prove that colleges can be repositories of knowledge available to all who seek larger perspectives on issues of concern or who simply want to engage in conversation on humanities topics of common interest. It bears repeating that universities are not the sole proprietors of the humanities; the cultural legacy belongs to all Alabamians, including those whose young-student days are far behind them. The writers drawn together in this volume show that the humanities are free to all with hearts and minds ready to respond to experience and to be uplifted by the humanistic forms that reflect and hold that experience. Each essay and story illustrates anew that no matter how dense our thickets may be, there are clearings that bring wisdom and delight. These clearings continue to be created in Alabama.

Three Perspectives

WAYNE FLYNT,
NORMAN BRITTIN
AND JOHN KUYKENDALL

The Alabama History and Heritage Festival proved—if proof is needed—that there is no barrier between the humanities in the academic community and the interests of the rest of the world. When the festival opened in Auburn in January 1983 all of the participating universities, agencies, and private groups were represented. Humanities-minded citizens from across the state were specially invited guests at the two-day conference. In addition to defining the humanities, displaying contributions made by Alabamians, and providing an opportunity for participants to discuss humanities projects with members of the Committee for the Humanities in Alabama, the conference offered three distinct perspectives on the humanities. Professors set the tone for the meeting—not by parading their special scholarship but by speaking to the fundamental questions that give rise to humanities studies. These three brief essays demonstrate that the humanities embrace our past, our distinctive language, and our search for meaning in life's events. Emerging from these personal reflections are perspectives on three humanities—history, English, and religious studies. The authors are Wayne Flynt, the chairman of Auburn's history department, Norman Brittin, professor emeritus of English, and John Kuykendall, then chairman of Auburn's religion department and now president of Davidson College.

Old Ways, Old Places
and Especially Old Stories
Once Bored Me to Tears

EACH YEAR ON THE SUNDAY before Labor Day my wife's family holds its annual reunion. Bearing many last names now—Brown, House, Smith, Flynt—the families come from near and far to the now nonexistent community of Brownsville in Clay County. There they gather at Hatchett Creek Presbyterian Church, a church to which the Browns originally belonged, founded in the early nineteenth century. We eat one of those legendary Southern homecoming dinners where everybody brings their favorite dish and the tables groan beneath the load. Our shelter is a huge tabernacle behind the church built nearly a hundred years ago when this place sometimes hosted five thousand people who came to its camp meeting revivals, living in cabins on the hillsides. Inside the neat frame church are forty-two benches, also built nearly a century ago, all crafted from one gigantic pine tree.

Nearby is a well-kept cemetery where the bodily remains of many of my wife's ancestors rest. As I stroll through the cemetery on a hot September afternoon the past comes sharply back again. There are graves of early pioneers—people born in England, Scotland, or northern Ireland, who braved both a fierce ocean and a primitive wilderness to carve a civilization in the rolling mountains of east-central Alabama. There are children's graves, a testimony to the frightful rate of infant mortality. Men rest there who fought in the Revolutionary War to create a new nation and in the Civil War to sever Alabama from the nation. The slogans chiseled into the stone markers testify to their hope for a better life and their faith in a triumphant resurrection.

Over the years I have developed a deep affection for that place. Once, we joined my brother-in-law's family camping overnight in the grove of trees separating the two parts of the cemetery. The next morning the older boys seined bait and caught fish from Hatchett Creek while the younger children chased lizards among the grave stones. The place is so quiet, so peaceful, so filled with the past, that you can almost—not quite, but almost—stop time still and feel how it once was.

History has long since passed Brownsville. The church still stands, thanks to the efforts of a little band of faithful worshipers. A few white-haired old ones still live in houses scattered along Hatchett Creek. But even they know that history has passed them by.

Yet every time I return for a reunion I can't help but think how mightily the events of that little community have affected my own life. But for the fierce individualism and deep commitment to freedom that these pioneers and others like them brought from Europe, there would have been no America. But for the hardships of clearing land and planting crops, there would have been no Alabama. But for the abiding religious faith handed down from generation to generation, there would have been no churches. But for their sacrifices, there would have been no progress. But for those who once lived at Brownsville, I would have a different wife.

I have not always felt so strongly about places like Hatchett Creek or the people who once inhabited them. It is, I suppose, a characteristic of youth to hold the past in disdain, to think that everything worth knowing is still to be learned, and that anyone over thirty is mentally fossilized. Old ways, old places, and especially old stories (already heard twenty times or more anyway) once bored me to tears. Passing the time with cousins my own age made visits to grandparents tolerable, and every now and then some quaint or bizarre practice even made such visits exciting. (I still remember most vividly the outdoor toilets and my grandmother wringing the necks of chickens.) But as soon as I became a teenager, with friends and activities of my own, I usually found an excuse to stay home and I thoroughly disengaged from my family's history. Only much later, when I began wondering why I was like I was, why I believed so strongly the things I believed, did I begin the long journey that led me back into my past. Like Alex Haley's search for his roots, sometimes the journey has become compulsive.

With William Faulkner, I have discovered that the past is not dead; in fact, it is not even past. So much of who we are as people depends on others—those who first came to this place, or who built the town we live in, the schools and churches we attend, those who made the sacrifices so we could have a better life.

The uses of the past are tremendously important. People who forget the past begin to take freedom for granted. They forget the frightful price which men and women paid to achieve and preserve liberty. We live in a time when barely half our citizens vote in presidential elections and fewer than that vote for governor. Our citizenry is too busy to work on community activities or to study carefully issues that face our nation.

The past can also reassure us. Although it is small comfort to someone out of a job, it is nonetheless important to remember that in the fall of 1932 twelve million Americans—nearly a third of the work force—were unemployed. And there was no unemployment compensation, no food stamps, or other forms of assistance. As tempted as we are sometimes to feel that we live in the worst of times, we need to remember a generation just now retiring that survived the Great Depression and the deadliest war in history. Our days are hard and they will make special demands on us, but those who came before us had problems just as bad.

History also reminds us that trouble is relative. Although the problems of the 1970s and 1980s are different from the 1950s and 1960s, I am not convinced that they are any worse. I will probably start a good argument over the question, but I will ask it anyway: Are the problems created by the prosperity and abundance of the 1950s and 1960s (materialism, status-seeking, a certain national arrogance of power, youth and adults spoiled by affluence, excessive leisure, loss in pride of workmanship) any more severe than the problems of our time (uncertainty about the future, financial distress, national self-doubt, unemployment)?

To be human means that we come to terms with history, and even the way we do so is controlled by the past. As a Southern historian I tend to confront the past not in abstraction but through specific places and concrete experiences—by way of Hatchett Creek churches. We can mythologize and distort the past, we can fight with it and denounce it, or we can lie down with it easily, wrap it around us as comfortably as a shawl before a roaring winter fire. The one thing we cannot do is escape its tenacious grasp.

—*Wayne Flynt*

**Language Enables Us to Take
Our Past along with Us—
Our Literature, Our History,
and All the Rest**

AT THE CLOSE of his essay, *A Defence of Poetry*, Shelley wrote: "Poets are the unacknowledged legislators of the world." The statement implies that, with their penetrative and prophetic powers, poets are in the vanguard of those who express the spirit of the age—or any age. The truths of poetry, Wordsworth said, are "carried alive into the heart by passion." Ever since prehistoric tribal times, far back in the shadowy world of oral tradition, poetry has been the center of what has come to be known as the humanities. For ages, poetry was the main vehicle for transmitting the knowledge of humankind—knowledge that, millennium after millennium, transformed our pithecanthropine ancestors into creatures undeniably human. With the advent of writing, prose came into being, but prose is a much later cultural development than poetry. Poetry is the heart of the humanities; it represents the oldest human feelings and the newest presentiments of human responses to inchoate patterns of existence.

Poetry and the other humanities—the literatures, histories, philosophies, and religions of the world—represent a vast body of knowledge and tradition that directly pertains to our permanent values. They comprise a corpus of cultural material, which until little more than a century ago constituted most of the curriculum in higher education and which still receives much attention even in our age of proliferating science and technology. Since the humanities emerge from the matrix of traditional values, they represent old and unifying knowledge. They chiefly give unity to a society.

Some may remember that back in 1959 C. P. Snow, later Lord Snow, the British physicist and novelist who lectured on The Two Cultures, lamented the division between the scientific culture and the traditional culture of the humanities, decrying the situation in which it is practically impossible to have meaningful communication between those people trained in science and those trained in the humanities. Snow believed that since scientists generally have a more forward-looking attitude and are more concerned with ameliorating the human condition than are the representatives of the "traditional culture," it is a pity that scientists have little political power—a power that still rests mainly in the hands of those not trained in science. But because science is not concerned with human values, except for that of Truth, I can hardly see how matters could be altered. The profession of politics is a very long way from being reduced to processes of quantification. An article in *Forbes* magazine criticized business management that takes only numbers into consideration. We are familiar with similar criticism of such "management" on the Auburn campus, and the two American presidents who came nearest to a scientific approach to governmental affairs—Hoover and Carter—were not conspicuously successful. Attention to human values lies at the heart of the institutions of our society, including politics.

But there is no denying the divisions in our culture. The vast amounts of new knowledge, scientific and technological, which are inundating us, are creating new vocations, ever more specialized specializations. New knowledge fragments our society, atomizes it. But the old knowledge, which pertains to our human values, our aspirations and failures and successes, indeed, the whole network of human relations, provides a cementing, unifying bond.

In several important ways, literature is the greatest of the humanities. Great literature is, first of all, universal; Aristotle said that poetry is "a more philosophical and a higher thing than history; for poetry tends to express the universal, history the particular." To the same purport is Thomas Love Peacock's tribute to "Shakespeare and his contemporaries, who used time and locality merely because they could not do without them, because every action must have its when and where." But literature surpasses journalistic when-and-where because literature creates and works through symbols—through characters and situations that achieve symbolic value. From the earliest heroes who caught and held the Western imagination—Homer's Hector and Achilles in the *Iliad*—to the bedeviled soldier in a more recent war—Yossarian of *Catch-22*—memorable figures of literature such as these stand for more than their individual selves, represent more than any actual human being, taking on a life beyond life through their symbolic proportions. Shakespeare's Falstaff, of course, is of their company, and Hamlet, and King Lear and Cordelia. Two of the greatest are Don Quixote and Sancho Panza. Moliere's Alceste and Tartuffe belong with them, as well as Arthur and Guienevere of Arthurian romance and, on our side of the water, Cooper's Leatherstocking and that shrewd and tenderhearted youngster, Huckleberry Finn.

But ballads and epics, stories, novels, and dramas do not merely present portraits of characters. What gives imaginative literature its deep appeal is that it illustrates character under pressure. The decisions that characters are required to make in matters of life and death in the face of some ominously looming deadline—with all that has happened earlier pressing upon them, forcing a fateful decision that could not have been made before that moment—reveal elements of their character and also determine their fates. Early in Act II of Shakespeare's *Julius Caesar*, Brutus decides to murder his best friend. And though assailed by temptation, Macbeth asserts: "We will proceed no further in this business"; but fifty lines later he has agreed to his wife's plan: "I am settled, and bend up/ Each corporal agent to this terrible feat." Mark Antony, having made a political marriage, declares, "I will to Egypt. . . ./ I' th' East my pleasure lies:" and he leaves Octavia, who is called "holy, cold, and still" to join Cleopatra, for "Age cannot wither her, nor custom stale/ Her infinite variety." And after Octavius Caesar has defeated Antony, Cleopatra too makes her final decision: suicide rather than the ignominy of being a spectacle in Caesar's triumph. Similarly, of course, thousands of literary figures choose otherwise—with Robert Jordan in Hemingway's *For Whom the Bell Tolls* and with Huck Finn, who, rather than betray his friend Nigger Jim, decides: "Well, then I'll *go* to hell!"

Actually, literature concerns every manifestation of human life. During the last two centuries numerous densely peopled literary worlds have been created: that of Scott and Dickens, of Balzac, Zola, Proust, Dostoyevsky and Tolstoy, of Jane Austen, Sigrid Undset, Eudora Welty, and William Faulkner, all constructing their world within one county. All such works of these writers, the poets, and the dramatists are achievements in language; whatever happens, whatever affect a reader experiences, happens through words. Let me remind you that language is man's greatest achievement; it is language that has given us preeminence over all the other animals; it is language that has made possible our culture and that whole incremental body of knowledge that we transmit generation after generation, including both science and history. But the words of science are not "carried alive into the heart by passion."

Literature deals with every manifestation of human life. I lack time to consider the phenomenon of style, but the linguistic choices resulting in effective literary word patterns represent differing styles appropriate to different occasions.

> The quality of mercy is not strained;
> It droppeth as the gentle rain from heaven
> Upon the place beneath. It is twice blest;
> It blesseth him that gives and him that takes.

Both vowel and consonant sounds recur in such ways that they are easy and pleasant to recite. But when King Lear, unmercifully rejected by his elder daughters and suffering the "impetuous blasts" of the tempest, launches his invective, the style is much different.

> Blow, winds, and crack your cheeks. Rage, Blow.
> You cataracts and hurricanes, spout
> Till you have drenched our steeples, drowned the cocks.

One of the qualities that gives Shakespeare supremacy among poets is his capacity for effective stylistic variation. But of course, choices of words (and rhythms) that give surprising precision to poetry constitute a large part of the glorious tradition in English through Milton, Pope, Keats, Tennyson, Frost, and Edna St. Vincent Millay.

On the basis of what I have said, my conclusions will not surprise you. Language is man's greatest invention. Literature is one of man's oldest and most exceptional cultural achievements. Language enables us to take our past along with us—our literature, our history, and all the rest. What does it mean to be human? To be human is to have a past. To be human is to read. To be human is to respond to the humanities.

—*Norman A. Brittin*

To be Human Means to Live With Our Feet on the Ground and Our Heads in the Heavens

TO SAY THAT RELIGION is a part of the humanities is to acknowledge that religion has been a part of human experience in virtually all times and all cultures. It is to acknowledge that there is a tendency innate to the human spirit to identify the sacred or the holy, both within our lives and beyond our lives, as a point star for meaning or purpose in existence. Admittedly, studying religion as a part of the humanities is *not* the same thing as studying religion as a means to growth in personal faith, although the one is certainly not inimical to the other. By studying religion we acknowledge the impact and value of a variety of faith commitments upon the lives of all sorts and conditions of people, in all sorts of personal and social circumstances.

The vantage of my discipline thus implies a number of things that are basic to our self-understanding as humans. Let me try, through the use of five mental snapshots, or images, to show you some of the most significant insights into the meaning of humanness that are provided by the study of religion.

Snapshot One: A new parent looking through the hospital glass at an infant and pondering the prospects for this fresh life.

To be human means to be able to ask the basic questions of life—questions like "whence" and "whither" and "why"—that remind us of both the things that we know and the things that we can only hope to know. It means to be able to ask the personal and corporate questions of origin and destiny and purpose, deriving some satisfaction from the questions, even when the answers are far from clear. There is meaning—perhaps even comfort—in the old saw that "A cow dies, but a person *has* to die." We know ourselves as creatures of consciousness, concerned about our nature and destiny in a way quite distinctive among all living things. The study of religion abets our efforts to ask such basic questions about life.

Snapshot Two: A solitary monk pondering the mystery that surrounds the object of his faith.

To be human means to be able to appreciate the significance of a realm beyond our senses. It means to be sensitive to the fact that this world that surrounds us, the essence of which we can see, hear, touch, taste, and smell, is an entity that points beyond itself. The world never claims to be altogether self-explanatory; it rather confronts us, in a variety of ways and occasions, as sacrament, as visible expression of invisible graciousness. Further, the awareness of this sacramental possibility in life also implies an openness to the experience of wonder. If this world has the potential to be an earnest of a realm unseen, it can evoke from us the sort of response that goes beyond mere pain or pleasure. It runs to mystery. To be human means to have the capacity to be overwhelmed.

Snapshot Three: A freshman, looking ahead at life through the gates of a college campus, seeking a match between talent and opportunity.

To be human means to be willing to ponder the possibility that life has been patterned or destined by a force beyond ourselves. It means to be willing to acknowledge intentionality or purpose in our experiences, however random or painful they may be at times. It means to be open to the experience of ultimate dependence, believing that as humans we have not only the right to freedom, but the opportunity of fitting into some larger scheme, under the guidance of a force that permeates the whole order of existence.

Snapshot Four: A middle-aged person toting up the list of accomplishments and failures in life and examining the meaning of the word "success."

To be human means to be willing to face realistically both the inclination to imperfection and the aspiration to perfection in the life of the human family and in our own lives. It means to know ourselves as we are, warts and all; but also to know our selves as we might become, with that rare, exclusively human capacity to let our reach exceed our grasp. From our own autobiographies and from the biographies of all who are kin to us in this *homo sapiens* clan, we know both the foibles and the fortunes of being human. We learn to be that strange combination of dissatisfaction and contentment, never willing to settle for mediocrity, yet knowing that "the best you can" is often/always flawed by who you are.

Snapshot Five: A bereaved spouse, smiling through tears of grief, recalling the delight of life together as husband and wife.

To be human means to have both a sense of the tragic and a sense of humor. It means to be willing to live between tears and laughter, often flinching at the profundity of evil and suffering in the midst of life, yet never allowing such pain to eradicate the joyous grin that comes also from the very heart of things. We make our beds in unfortunate places and find that we must lie in them; yet the sun that bids us rise reminds us that "Light is sweet" and that our days are made for song as well as sorrow. So we can weep and we can chuckle, and we can sense a certain incompleteness in those who cannot do both.

To wit, to be human—in my area of the humanities and the others, too, I'd venture—means to be able to live with our feet on the ground and our heads in the heavens. It means to live as creatures who know at once the grit and the grandeur of life, and see both as a part of a pattern that we can ultimately neither control nor comprehend. It means to see in the lives and works of others, and in our own life and work, glimpses of truth (capital T if you wish) that illumine the rest of the way.

—John W. Kuykendall

Romance and

High Adventure

HARPER LEE

Alabama's best-known fiction writer, winner of a Pulitzer Prize for *To Kill A Mockingbird*, made a rare public appearance in Eufaula in March of 1983 to participate in the Alabama History and Heritage Festival. No one suggested a topic to her, but the paper that Harper Lee presented to that gathering—published here in its entirety—provided a perfect illustration of the festival's theme. Alabama's history is charged with drama and meaning, but who cares nowadays? Who reads Albert Pickett, the writer to whom all students of Alabama history owe a debt? And what is there for those who do seek the drama of nineteenth-century Alabama? What did Pickett see in Sam Dale, Jere Austill, Caesar the slave, and those warring Creeks in the great canoe fight? Obviously the fullness of Albert Pickett's work is not lost on Harper Lee. As a fiction writer who has observed the turbulence of her own century and its effect on a small Alabama town, she is aware that history is a seamless garment. Her ability to define characters such as Scout and Jem against the backdrop of Alabama history may be one reason why twelve million copies of her novel have been sold. With swift authority Harper Lee does more in this essay than simply present to us a quaint and forgotten fragment of our past. She pricks our conscience and reminds us—yet again— that history is a living creature, waiting to be noticed.

ALBERT JAMES PICKETT was born in 1810, in Anson County, North Carolina, and moved with his family to what is now Autauga County, Alabama, in 1818, where his father established a plantation and trading-house. He received a "gentleman's education," which meant a military academy in Connecticut and Stafford County Academy in Virginia. In 1830 he returned home. Although he acquired extensive acreage in the vicinity of his father's plantation, Pickett was no farmer. Agriculture, he said, "did not occupy one-fourth of my time. Having no taste for politics, and never having studied a profession, I determined to write a history." It was lucky for us that he did.

After spending more than seventeen years collecting the material, Pickett began writing his *History of Alabama* in 1847. It was published in 1851 and, after having gone through several editions to 1900, was out of print until 1962, when it was republished as a sort of historical curiosity.

We Americans like to put our culture into disposable containers. Nowhere is this more evident than in the way we treat our past. We discard villages, towns, even cities, when they grow old, and we are now in the process of discarding our recorded history, not in a shredder, but by rewriting it as romance. We are eager to watch docu-dramas on television; we prefer to read a history of the American Revolution as seen through the eyes of Mad Anthony Wayne's last mistress. Now there is nothing wrong in reading historical fiction—perhaps two-thirds of the world's classics are written in that form. But these are impatient days; more than ever it seems that we want anything but the real thing: we are afraid that the real thing might be dull, demanding, and worst of all, lacking in suspense.

So it gives me the greatest pleasure to remind the members of my own generation (who have all read it) and report to the younger ones among us, that although it's the real thing, Pickett's *History of Alabama* is a work so fraught with romance and high adventure that even John Jakes would sit up and take notice.

In what would occupy a few paragraphs of an American history survey, Pickett took 669 pages to unfold a story that is more hair-raising than anything yet seen on television. Indeed, in today's terms, it is almost as though Pickett trained a camera in relentless, unblinking close-up on a period of Alabama history that we seldom think about any more, a period that sometimes seems to live only in our place-names and on roadside markers. (Where was Maubila? On the Tombigbee somewhere? Where was Tookabatcha? On the Coosa, or was it the Tallapoosa? Maybe it was on the Alabama. These were the names of separate and distinct peoples, with their own history.)

In a prose style that falls somewhere between Macaulay and Bulwer-Lytton, Pickett's history opens with a blood-curdling account of Hernando DeSoto's progress through our state, in which he destroyed nearly everything in his path, including the Mobilians and their giant chief, Tuscaloosa, the Black Warrior.

Had he been a modern historian, Pickett would have gone straight on from there, but "as our soil remained untrodden by European feet for nearly a century and a half," Pickett passed the time between DeSoto and the arrival of the French with five chapters of what makes for compulsive reading. In a long digression describing the native inhabitants of what is now Alabama, Georgia, and Mississippi, he wrote a miniature social history that can hold its own with any modern work. For these chapters alone, I think Pickett deserves a place in American literature.

We meet them all, but the most prominent tribes were the ferocious, insolent Chickasaws, who put paid to DeSoto somewhere in Mississippi; the silver-tongued Choctaws, who could not swim, who were unaggressive when not defending their own turf, and who were notable even among their own kind for their revolting burial practices. In the northeast were the comparatively genial Cherokees, and in the west the aristocratic, despotic Natchez. On center stage were the Muscogees, later known as the Creeks, who, after pushing into the state in the vacuum created by DeSoto, formed a confederation with the Alabamas and remnants of the shattered smaller tribes. Pickett's history is essentially the story of the Creeks and the people who destroyed them.

The Creeks were a remarkable people. Their social and political structure was as complex as anything in Europe, and in some ways was far more advanced than that of the earliest settlers. Divorce, for example, was at the choice of either party and with only a slight advantage to the man: he could remarry immediately, but the woman had to wait until The Green Corn Dance was over. "Marriage," said Pickett, "gave no right to the husband over the property of the wife, or the control or management of the children he might have by her." Adultery, however, was another matter. The pains and penalties for that sport rendered its practice infrequent.

They were a gregarious people. "Their most manly and important game was 'the ball play'," said Pickett; it seemed to be a version of lacrosse. The warriors of one town challenged those of another, and "for several days previous to the time, those who intended to engage in the amusement took medicine, as though they were going to war." In the presence of multitudes, the players "rushed together with a mighty shock . . . were often severely hurt, and sometimes killed, in the rough and unfeeling scramble which prevailed. . . . In the meantime, the women were constantly on the alert with vessels and gourds filled with water, watching every opportunity to supply the players. It sometimes happened that the inhabitants of a town gamed away all their ponies, jewels, and wearing apparel. . . ." Does that sound familiar? Every fall and winter weekend finds today's Alabamians at similar pursuits.

Their religion, an integral part of everything that they did, was so complicated and structured as to delight the heart of a pharisee. Indeed, Pickett delights *us* with the theories of one James Adair, who lived among the Indians for more than thirty years and emerged from the forest in 1775 with an enormous volume that sought to prove that the Creeks and their neighbors were in fact Jews. After observing the intricate similarities of the two religions, the clincher for Adair was in watching the warriors dance "around the holy fire, during which the elder priest invoked the Great Spirit, while the others responded *Halelu! Halelu!* then *Haleluiah! Haleluiah!"*

Pickett's narrative of the sufferings, struggles, and massacres of the early colonists, the gradual opening of the region to commerce, the various wars and alliances of the three greedy powers—Britain, France, and Spain—is one of fascinating detail. We follow the fortunes of the Sieur de Bienville, who must have been appointed governor of the French colony by mistake, because he was a decent, incorruptible and, on the whole, benevolent man. Along the way we meet the English General James Oglethorpe and his philanthropical experiment in Georgia, and incidentally get a glimpse of John and Charles Wesley. We meet schemers, rogues, and vagabonds; scores of minor characters come alive on the pages—one elegant lady on the razzle in the wilderness, claiming to be the Tsar of Russia's sister-in-law; the valiant Beaudrot, for whom many Southerners are named, but don't know exactly why; the Jewish trader Abram Mordecai, who spent fifty years in the wilderness and had his ear cut off for amorous dalliance with a married squaw.

Through the years, when the Indians felt too much pressure from the constant encroachments of the Europeans, they always responded to broken promises with savage violence, until there appeared among the Creeks their greatest chieftain, Alexander McGillivray, who led them to the high-watermark of their history. The story of McGillivray and his family should be so familiar to all Alabamians that I shall not repeat it, but say that if the Creeks ever had a chance to survive as a nation, they had it with him. Yet in the seventeen years of his spectacular leadership, McGillivray showed his feet of clay—his intrigues with the brand-new American government and with the Spanish authorities in Florida, for his personal aggrandizement, set the Creeks on a collision course with extinction.

The Indians hated the new Americans even more than they hated the British, French, and Spanish—there were more of them. The second Yazoo Land Sale (the first was a fizzle) resulted in more settlers coming in as never before—this time under the protection of the American government.

The Americans established outposts and small forts on Alabama's rivers, cleared the forests, and gradually created a recognizable society in the wilderness, sometimes marrying the descendants of the first settlers who had married Indians. Many of the oldest families in Alabama can proudly point to their Indian heritage.

Now a note of warning—when we think of Alabama history we think of slavery and we should. In 1540 when DeSoto arrived with his slaves, he found the Indians enslaving each other; when the French first imported African slaves, the Africans were bought by prosperous Indians or captured as prizes in raids. In 1847 when Pickett began to write his history, slavery was a fact of life and he treats it as such, so don't be shocked. Slavery, you still remember, is man's oldest institution, and its abolition is the only fundamental moral change that Western man has yet made.

Well, just when everybody was settling in and government agents were helping manage Indian affairs, the United States and Britain went to war. The Indians had given permission for the new Federal Road to cut through the heart of their territory, which meant even more emigrants, and the Creeks, said Pickett, "with their usual sagacity, foresaw that they would soon be hemmed in by the Georgians on one side and the Tombigbee people on the other." The Spanish to the south hated the emigrants also. British agents, operating in Canada and as guests of the Spanish in Pensacola, urged the Creeks to come in on their side against the Americans, and from Detroit they sent to Alabama an evangelist I can only describe as a direct ancestor of the Ayatolla Khomeini.

Chief Tecumseh, a Shawnee of national renown as a warrior, and his chief prophet descended upon Creek villages preaching fire and revolution. Pickett's description of their performance at the Creek capital, Tookabatcha, at a grand council of the Indians, is spine-chilling. Here is a summary of Tecumseh's remarks: return to your primitive customs, throw away the plough and the loom; become warriors again; stay away from the grasping unprincipled white race; when they've cut down your beautiful forests and stained your clear rivers, they will subject you to African servitude; dress again in the skins of beasts, use the war club, the scalping knife, and the bow; drive them out and destroy them.

Tecumseh's chief prophet was also busy. He established a soothsaying college and turned out local prophets trained in new and potent magic. Although the rank and file drank the magic brew eagerly, the Big Warrior at Tookabatcha was skeptical. Tecumseh said, "You do not mean to fight. I know the reason. You do not believe the Great Spirit has sent me. You shall believe it. . . . I shall go straight to Detroit. When I get there I will stamp my foot upon the ground and shake down every house in Tookabatcha."

The common Indians, said Pickett, believed every word of Tecumseh's threat, and they counted the days it took Tecumseh to reach Detroit. "One day," said Pickett, "a mighty rumbling was heard in the earth, the houses of Tookabatcha reeled and tottered, and reeled again." As if a fortuitous earthquake were not enough, the British at Pensacola provided a further incentive to war: they offered the Indians $10 a scalp.

The Red Sticks—the war party, the fundamentalists—went on the rampage throughout Alabama. Creek families were divided (not the least of which was the family of Alexander McGillivray) and they fought each other as well as the Americans. It was not until after the massacre at Fort Mims, led by McGillivray's nephew, William Weatherford, that help came from the north.

Andrew Jackson with his Tennesseans at Talladega and General Claiborne in the south at the Holy Ground—where, incidentally, Alexander McGillivray's sister was found tied to a stake surrounded by a lightwood fire, and where her nephew, Weatherford, who had put her there, made his famous escape—were engagements that began to spell the end, which came, as we all know, in a few furious hours at Horseshoe Bend in Tallapoosa County.

Tecumseh's revival meeting at Tookabatcha resulted in the Creeks losing nearly one-half of what is now Alabama, and their eventual removal from the state.

Pickett ended his history with the admission of Alabama to the Union in 1819. "To some other person," he said, "fonder than we are of the dry details of state legislation and fierce party spirit, we leave the task of bringing the history down to a later period."

But I wonder if that was his reason. I think Pickett left his heart at Horseshoe Bend. I do not believe that it was in him to write of the eventual fate of the Creek Nation, of the Cherokees, of the Chickasaws and Choctaws, which was decided well within his own lifetime.

Pickett's *History of Alabama*, this unique treasure, now lies hidden in old family bookcases, has been discarded by libraries, sometimes turns up in rummage sales, and is certainly not used in our schools. In my opinion it should be in every high school library in the state.

I have no idea what today's historians think of Albert Pickett—very little, I should guess, for Pickett's history is composed of small dramas within a huge drama, much of it drawn from the memories of those who were there, from individuals whose bravery and sacrifice created the state of Alabama. Modern research techniques and professionally objective evaluations were unknown to Pickett, as they were unknown to his contemporaries Macaulay and Prescott, but then who reads them any more?

The First Creek War:

Twilight

of Annihilation

JOHN W. COTTIER

AND GREGORY A. WASELKOV

A narrative exists in time and time exists before our recorded histories. In a continuation of the story that Albert Pickett first told, archaeologists John Cottier and Gregory Waselkov supply physical evidence of this drama from artifacts, documents, and their own research. Their research further explains the cultural changes that took place from the late prehistoric to early historic periods of central Alabama when the Creek Indians were the primary culture. In this essay, the two humanities scholars set the stage for a major historical change—the coming of the white culture and the destruction of the red. Both of these archaeologists have done primary Alabama research. Waselkov has conducted excavations at the sites of Fort Toulouse and Fort Jackson, near Montgomery; Cottier's recent projects include excavations at an early French colonial site at Mobile and survey investigations along the lower Alabama River. One indication of the breadth of their research—and one reflection of the working life of the modern archaeologist—is the array of granting agencies supporting their pursuits. Some of the information in the following essay came from investigations supported in part by the Alabama Historical Commission, the National Park Service, Auburn University's Faculty Grant-in-Aid Program, the National Science Foundation, and the Mobile District Office of the U.S. Army Corps of Engineers. As they show how one culture's death signaled the arrival of another, the authors cite several historical sources, among them Albert Pickett. Their notations refer to a bibliography published at the conclusion of the essay; readers interested in early Alabama history will want to consult these texts further.

AFTER THE WITHDRAWAL of the French from the Alabama River Valley in 1764 until the first decade of the nineteenth century, the Creek and Alabama Indians managed to resist encroachments of white settlers. By skillfully playing the British and Spanish, and later the Americans, against one another, the Creeks retained possession of most of their lands. However, the rapidly expanding population of the young United States eventually threatened Indian sovereignty of all lands east of the Mississippi River, as well as those of nearby European colonies. The Louisiana Purchase of 1803 sparked a movement among western and southern settlers to expand the boundaries of the United States. Spain's weakly held colonies to the south were tempting targets for American filibusters, with abortive uprisings occurring at Baton Rouge and Pensacola in 1810. But not until the outbreak of war with Great Britain in 1812 was the United States government willing to attempt conquests in Spanish West Florida. Considering the expansionist climate of the period, the Creeks were wary of further demands on their rightfully held lands and found diverse support for this position. While its causes were numerous, the ensuing Creek War of 1813-1814 was an important event in the history of the South and forever changed this region.

Background to Hostilities

By the early 1800s some individuals were settling on Indian lands, and several attempts were made to extend the Georgia frontier into the Creek's country. White settlements in the forks of the lower Alabama and Tombigbee rivers also increased. Various routes were followed by those immigrants, some coming overland along Indian trails from the north and east. Responding to this traffic, Samuel Mims established a ferry across the Alabama, which, along with Hollinger's ferry on the Tombigbee, provided the first such services on these rivers (Hamilton, 1898: 49). By 1804 plans were established to create a horse path from the Ocmulgee to the Mobile through Indian country. The Treaty of Washington in 1805 not only contained an extensive Creek land cession, but also authorized the United States to maintain this horse path across the Creek lands, provided the Indians would maintain ferries and rest stops (Doster, 1974: 1:243).

This Federal Road was utilized almost immediately. Its course entered present-day Alabama just south of what is today Columbus, Georgia, and continued to the Tombigbee settlements by the cutoff and over Mims's and Hollinger's ferries (Owen, 1911; Cooke, 1935). A later branch of this road also crossed the Alabama River at Weatherford's Bluff (later called Claiborne) and continued to St. Stephens; following this expansion, another route was opened along the east side of the Alabama River to the Tensaw Lake settlements and on to Blakeley and Mobile. By 1810 white settlements had increased substantially in the forks area of the Alabama and Tombigbee rivers, and an additional ferry was in operation across the Alabama River just above its junction with the Little River. The road was improved and widened by military troops in 1811 despite strong protests from the Creeks (Cotterill, 1954: 162); an invasion of settlers quickly moved southward along this wagon road.

The impact of this trail across Indian lands and the settlements that developed along it have been suggested as being significant sources of conflict between the natives and the whites. However, the road was only one exacerbation of conditions that were generally present as a result of the continued acculturation of the Creeks (Nunez, 1958). Numerous notes of discord had previously been raised by the Creeks in their associations with the Federal government (Doster, 1974: 2:11-12), and some of this conflict was tempered by the personal ambitions and greed of the principal Upper Creek chiefs. Likewise, while many of the Lower Creeks were rapidly adopting certain aspects of the Georgian plantation way of life, many of the Upper Creeks attempted to maintain more traditional ways of life. These Creeks also had long claimed and exercised hunting rights in a large area north of the Tennessee River and had bitterly resisted white settlement in middle Tennessee (Doster, 1974: vol. 2).

Throughout the years 1809-1811, the continuation of these unresolved problems especially concerned the Upper Creeks. Intrusions and encroachments by whites continued, and in 1809 Hoboheilthle Micco (Tame King of Tallassee and the Speaker for the Nation) notified President Thomas Jefferson of such violations and indicated "the Muscogee land is becoming very small. . . . When a thing begins to grow scarce it is natural to love it. . . . I hope you will think I have told you right what land we have left we cannot spare, and you will find we are distressed" (Doster, 1974: 2:16). Both Jefferson and Benjamin Hawkins, United States Indian agent to the Creeks, continued to stress a paternalistic policy of civilization for their charges.

The impact of culture change, however, created threats that were not perceptible to those involved. Not only was there division between the Upper and Lower Creeks, but also growing fragmentation among the Upper Creeks. Principal complaints concerned the distribution of trade stipends, the opening of roads and river traffic across Creek country, questions of a constitutional and governmental nature, and the continued erosion of Creek control over their own lands. The crisis was real and friction continued to estrange the Creeks.

In September of 1811, some five thousand Creeks gathered at the town of Tuckabatchee to hear Tecumseh, a Shawnee leader, speak of a new religion. In his address to the Creek Council, Tecumseh advocated, in somewhat mysterious talk, revival of old Indian ways and rejection of all things foreign. As Benjamin Hawkins later related, the covert meaning of such talk was to:

> Kill the old chiefs, friends to peace; kill the cattle, the hogs, and fowls; do not work, destroy the wheels and looms, throw away your ploughs, and every thing used by the Americans. Sing "the song of the Indians of the northern lakes, and dance their dance." Shake your war clubs, shake yourselves; you will frighten the Americans, their arms will drop from their hands, the ground will become a bog, and mire them, and you may knock them on the head with your war clubs. I will be with you with my Shawanese, as soon as our friends the British are ready for us. Lift up the war club with your right hand, be strong, and I will come and show you how to use it. (Hawkins's letter to Big Warrior, et al. Lowrie and Clarke, 1832: 845)

Overimaginative accounts have also unduly associated Tecumseh's appeal to the Creeks with natural signs of comets and earthquakes, while also suggesting a mnemonic calendar of bundles of small red sticks. A comet and an earthquake (the New Madrid earthquake of 1811-1812) perhaps did influence some Creeks, but the discarding of a stick each day to coordinate their war efforts seems unreconcilable with the basic calendrical knowledge of the Creeks and the actual events of the war.

Tecumseh's message and the prophetic-nativistic activity which it inspired are examples of what anthropologists have termed "revitalization movements." Such movements have often occurred when traditional cultures become drastically disrupted by western colonization. In this case, Creek society attempted to resolve conflicts that arose in a world so altered by the presence of white men that their traditional Indian value system was no longer relevant. Tecumseh offered mystical powers that would enable the Creeks to rid their world of the Euro-American threat to their existence. The nativistic attempt of the Creeks conveyed a strong religious flavor. This is especially poignant in the accounts of George Stiggins, U.S. Creek Indian agent from 1831 to 1844 (Nunez, 1958). General James Wilkinson even reported:

> To effect the object at which they aim, they have had recourse to religious imposture. One Joseph Francis, who lived on the road,

pretends he has had a visit from the Lord, who has revealed many things to him, which are shaped and detailed in the manner most impressive on his barbarian auditors. But in aid of superstitious awe manual force is employed to convert the obdurate and unenlightened (quoted by Claiborne, 1880: 322).

Similar scenarios were played out in the Ghost Dance of the Indians of the Great Plains and in the Earth Lodge and Bole Maru cults of the Pacific Northwest coast (Mooney, 1965; Wallace, 1956).

Tecumseh's proselytizing left the Creeks further divided and unsure of the best course to follow. The Lower Creeks, who lived in closest proximity to white settlers, were more strongly influenced by Benjamin Hawkins and the government's "civilizing policy" (Wallace, 1972: 219). For almost twenty years, Hawkins had encouraged domestic husbandry, fencing and plowing of fields, home cloth production, and a reorganization of the Creek political organization, which would give more public authority to the headman and put a national council under his control (Sheehan, 1973: 141-42; Pound, 1951). He had defended Creek rights by attempting to remove intruding settlers and cattle from their lands and had gained the confidence of many of the Lower Creeks (Pound, 1951: 161; Prucha, 1962: 158). Perhaps because they were not in such direct contact with encroaching white settlers and could thus view with some detachment the deleterious effects that such contact had on the Lower Creeks, the Alabamas and most Upper Creeks repudiated Hawkins's civilizing policy; they were more willing to accept Tecumseh's new religion and took great hope in its promises.

One immediate source of conflict between the Creeks and Americans stemmed from demands by Tennesseans desiring to market their produce in Mobile; they demanded that the Coosa River be opened to white navigation. The Upper Creeks were extremely alarmed at this new proposal, fearing that the whiskey trade, which would inevitably accompany the river traffic, would bring ruin on their people (Lowrie and Clarke, 1832: 845).

The Creek War, 1813-1814

For whatever specific reasons, early in 1813 several Red Sticks, members of the pro-war faction, murdered eight white settlers in western Georgia and the Ohio country. Hawkins pressured the Creek chiefs to capture and deliver to him the guilty warriors. The chiefs exercised their still considerable influence to have the murderers pursued; they would not surrender and all were killed (Doster, 1974: 2:69-71). This display of allegiance to the United States Indian agent deepened the rift between the Red Sticks and the headmen's factions and led to revenge killings of some headmen and their followers (Lowrie and Clarke, 1832: 849-50). By mid-year, the pro-American chiefs realized the extent of dissatisfaction among the Creeks and the growing power and prestige of certain Red Stick "prophets." These prophets were present in growing numbers among both the Upper Creeks and the Alabamas, the latter of whom Hawkins patronizingly characterized as:

> the most industrious and best behaved of all our Indians. Their fields were the granary of the upper towns, and furnished considerable supplies, by water, to Mobile. But this fanaticism has rendered them quite the reverse (Lowrie and Clarke, 1832: 847).

The prophets' influence quickly spread throughout most Upper Creek towns and the direction of their movement soon became clear. Alexander Cornells, an interpreter for Hawkins, reported that "the prophets are enemies to the plan of civilization and advocates for the wild Indian mode of living" (Lowrie and Clarke, 1832: 846). Hawkins commented on this fanaticism on 27 June 1813 and correctly speculated:

> If it could confine itself to a contest among the chiefs of power, and not interfere with the friendly relations between the Creek nation and the United States, it might be policy in us to look on, and let it be settled among themselves; but, as there seems to be another object coupled with it, and that of hostility to us eventually, we must be ready to apply a military corrective in due time (Lowrie and Clarke, 1832: 847).

On 5 July 1813, a party of Red Sticks burned the village of Hatchechubbau and destroyed cattle, hogs, horses, and corn. In addition, the town of Tuckabatchee was besieged by Red Sticks from other Upper Creek towns. Thus, a civil war had started among the Creeks. Hawkins took a lead in this conflict and indicated to General Armstrong, United States Secretary of War, that he had "advised the council, repeatedly, to order a party to attack and destroy the prophets, without delay, but they seem not equal, in their present state of alarm and confusion, to such an enterprise" (Lowrie and Clarke, 1832: 848). Later that month Hawkins sent a threat to the "fanatical chief" that "if the white man is in danger in your land, you are in danger; and war with the white people will be your ruin" (Lowrie and Clarke, 1832: 848).

However, the Indians were involved initially in a civil war and the Tame King stated: "I am not at war with any nations of people; I am settling an affair with my own chiefs" (Lowrie and Clarke, 1832: 849). Some of the basic Red Stick aims at this time appear to have been destruction of the towns of Tuckabatchee, Coweta, and Cussetah. Yet Hawkins also indicated:

> the declaration of the Prophets is, to destroy everything received from the Americans; all the chiefs and their adherents who are friendly to the customs and ways of the white people; to put to death every man who will not join them; and, by those means, to unite the nation in aid of the British, and Indians of the lakes, against their white neighbors, as soon as their friends, the British, will be ready for them (Lowrie and Clarke, 1832: 850).

The initial hostilities were merely a prelude to a massive attack on the Lower Creek town of Coweta, which was planned for August 1813. To prepare for this venture, several hundred Red Sticks under the leadership of Peter McQueen traveled to Pensacola, where the Spanish commandant reluctantly provided them with three hundred pounds each of powder and lead, and some firearms (Doster, 1974: 2:78-79; Boyd, 1937: 56-59; Halbert and Ball, 1969: 66-71). During this expedition, the Red Sticks terrorized mixed-bloods along their path and burned the home of James Cornells, brother of Alexander, and abducted James's wife. American settlers in the Lower Alabama River Valley hastily constructed defensive fortifications within the forks of the Alabama and Tombigbee rivers (Harris, 1977), and Governor David Holmes of the Mississippi Territory provided militia forces to aid in their support. As early as 1812, Colonel James Caller of the local militia had written the governor:

> there can be but little doubt but the creek indians intend making an attack on our frontiers and that they are waiting for a favorable op-

portunity to strike the blow from information received from indians and half breeds. . . . The settlers in the fork of the Alabama and
Tombigbee rivers are much alarmed and some have actually fled
from their homes. . . . Our frontiers are in a very defenseless situation. Many of the inhabitants are without arms and most of them
without ammunition. . . . We think there is not time to be lost in
putting our frontiers in as good a state of defense as possible. . . .
The settlers in the fork of Tombigbee and Alabama amounting to
nearly one half of the population property and respectability of the
Counties of Washington and Baldwin are settlers on the public
lands without any authority of government and from this circum-
stance we fear they would receive no support from the U.S. troops
here even were the indians to make an actual attack on them, as the
commanding officer at Fort Stoddert has in conversation expressed
doubt whether he would be authorized to protect this class of citizens without a positive order to that effect (Doster, 1974: 2:67).

When the settlers in the forks area heard reports of the Red
Sticks' visit to Pensacola, their militia rode east to intercept them.
At the ensuing Battle of Burnt Corn Creek on 27 July 1813, the
American militia, under Colonel Caller, had the initial advantage,
but was repulsed and retreated in disarray (Owsley, 1981: 30-32).
This defeat greatly alarmed the settlers within the forks. At the
same time, but to the north, Hawkins had attempted to attack the
Red Sticks with his Indian forces and had burned the deserted vil-
lage of Peter McQueen.

Perhaps surprised at American intervention at Burnt Corn
Creek in what had heretofore been a Creek civil war, the Red Stick
prophets decided to alter their plans. Three Upper Creek towns
were to form "a front of observation" toward Coweta to conceal the
true intent, which was an attack on the whites and pro-American
Indians within the forks of the Alabama and Tombigbee rivers.

The "Fort Mims Massacre," as it came to be known among the
whites, occurred around noon on 30 August 1813. The militia gar-
rison at this fort (actually a palisaded plantation house where local
settlers had gathered for protection) was ill-prepared for the well-
organized attack. When the battle ended, some 250 to 275 whites
and mixed-bloods, including many women and children, had been

killed and numerous black slaves captured. Only about 20 persons escaped (Owsley, 1981: 36-39). Although the Red Stick attack by warriors from thirteen towns had been a great tactical success, Creek losses were considerably higher than the two or three predicted by the prophets (Lowrie and Clarke, 1832: 852). More importantly, Americans were shocked at the news and plans were immediately made for a three-pronged attack on the Upper Creeks.

The proposal called for one army, composed of Mississippi volunteer militia and elements of the Third Regiment U.S. Infantry, under General Ferdinand L. Claiborne, brother of the governor of Louisiana, to move up the Alabama River and protect the American settlements north of Mobile. Another army led by Major General Andrew Jackson, commander of the Tennessee militia, was to march southward down the Coosa and upper Tallapoosa river valleys with two brigades of Tennessee militia and the 39th and 44th Regiments of U.S. Infantry. The third force, consisting of the Georgia volunteer militia and the balance of the Third Regiment (later reinforced by the Carolina Brigade) under the command of General John Floyd, was directed to advance along the Federal Road leading from the Chattahoochee to the Alabama River.

In spite of the imposing forces arrayed against them, the Upper Creeks vigorously, and for a time successfully, defended their country, receiving encouragement and supplies from British agents in Florida. Jackson's Tennessee Army made some initial progress at the battles of Tallussahatchee (3 November 1813) and Talladega (9 November 1813). On 18 November, the East Tennessee militia under General White attacked a Hillabee village that had recently surrendered to Jackson. The resultant massacre prompted the surviving Hillabees to fight unremittingly to the end of the war. After this brief campaign, Jackson was forced to return to his base at Fort Strother because of lack of supplies and a series of mutinies that dissolved his army. On the eastern front, the Georgia militia under Floyd attacked and burned Atassi (Autossee) on 29 November 1813, and Major General David Adams burned several Upper Creek towns including Nuyaka on 17 December 1813. After these forays, the Georgia militia retreated to Fort Mitchell.

To the south, General Claiborne was also occupied. In June 1813, he had been ordered to Fort Stoddert for the defense of the

Mobile settlements during the initial Indian scare. In the Tensaw River settlements, his militia was thinly spread; its largest contingent of about 120 men under Major Daniel Beasley was destroyed at Fort Mims (Owsley, 1981: 35). After the fall of Mims, additional militia was called to duty by Governor Holmes of the Mississippi Territory, and these units strengthened the somewhat fragile position of General Claiborne (Claiborne, 1880: 326). Likewise during this time, Claiborne consolidated American relationships with some of the other southeastern Indians, especially the Choctaws.

By October, Claiborne's army received orders to proceed to Weatherford's Bluff to establish a fort and depot. The army left St. Stephens and engaged in some limited action with small parties of hostile Creeks who had been harassing the Alabama River Valley settlers. As part of this movement, Captain Sam Dale and over seventy men moved up the river. On 12 November, just above Brazier's Landing (later French's Landing) and near Randon's Creek, the famous "canoe fight" occurred. In this skirmish, Dale, James Smith, Jeremiah Austill, and a slave named Caesar, paddling a dugout, killed nine Indians in a canoe and thus entered the pages of history as Alabama folk heroes (Halbert and Ball, 1969; Pickett, 1962).

On 17 November, Claiborne arrived at Weatherford's Bluff and constructed "a strong stockade, two hundred feet square, defended by three block houses and a half-moon battery, which commanded the river" (Halbert and Ball, 1969: 241-42). Claiborne summed up the situation:

> I am now on the east bank of the Alabama, thirty-five miles above Mims, and in the best part of the enemy's country. From this position we cut the savages off from the river, and from their growing crops. We likewise render their communication with Pensacola more hazardous. Here will be deposited for the use of General Jackson, a supply of provisions, and I hope I shall be ordered to co-operate with him. . . . We have by several excursions alarmed the Indians, and the possession of this important position will induce them to retire. I have with me Pushmataha, who, with fifty-one warriors, accompanied by Lieutenant Calahan of the volunteers, will march this morning and take up a position to intercept more effectually the communication of the enemy with Pensacola (Halbert and Ball, 1969: 242).

After its construction, Fort Claiborne at the American Heights remained a strategic location well after the Creek War. Likewise, the town that developed at the fort became an important river port later in the nineteenth century.

During the Creek War, only minor events transpired at Fort Claiborne. Some skirmishes occurred, including a night attack made by Pushmataha's Choctaws on a hostile Creek party near Burnt Corn Creek (Halbert and Ball, 1969: 242-43). General Claiborne's army was also strengthened to about 1,200 upon the arrival of Colonel Russell, Commander of Mount Vernon, with the Third Regiment U.S. Infantry (Owsley, 1981: 46-47). In December, this combined army marched north into the Red Stick territory to Fort Deposit in present Lowndes County. This established a fortified position along the Federal Road, which also placed Claiborne's army within thirty miles of the Indian town of Holy Ground.

Holy Ground, or Ecanachaga (sacred or beloved ground), was established by Josiah Francis, known as the Prophet Francis, or Hillis Hadjo (Crazy Medicine) (Nunez, 1958: 8). Francis indicated "the master of breath" had selected that location and consecrated it for sacred use by Indians only. Despite the prophet's contentions, the town was destroyed on 23 December 1813, along with several other Indian encampments. The destruction of Holy Ground was important, and, as Indian Agent George Stiggins later reported: "the burning of the Ecanachaga gave relief to the white people of the settlements down the river, it finally closed the hostile operations and incursions of magnitude of the lower towns Indians" (Nunez, 1958: 172). After the battle, Claiborne's army returned to their base at Fort Claiborne, and the majority were mustered out of the service. As a result of his poor health, General Claiborne retired to Natchez where he died in 1815 (Claiborne, 1880: 340). The removal of the Mississippi militia from the southern front left only Colonel Russell and a small force of about six hundred men of the Third Regiment active in the Lower Alabama River Valley.

The limited forces of Colonel Russell at Fort Claiborne were not to take significant offensive actions after Holy Ground. Instead, his unit was to provide logistical support via the river for actions in central Alabama (Owsley, 1981: 49). Russell did attempt to engage the Red Sticks along the Cahaba River in early February 1814. In this expedition, Captain James Dinkins went up the Alabama River by boat to rendezvous with Russell who had traveled overland. Due to imprecise information on the distances involved, these units never met; Russell depleted his provisions, burned deserted Red Stick towns, and made a forced march back to Fort Claiborne. In this ill-fated expedition, Russell also sent Lieutenant James M. Wilcox and a small party from the Cahaba towns down river to meet Dinkins and apprise him of the situation (Austill, 1923: 29; Owsley, 1981: 49-50). Lieutenant Wilcox was killed in an Indian ambush, but the remainder of the group reached Dinkins, who had mistakenly passed the Cahaba River and was now returning to Fort Claiborne (Pickett, 1962: 578). Wilcox County was later named for this officer, and the action that took his life may have occurred at the mouth of Pursley Creek (Hamilton and Owen, 1898: 154).

While activities lulled along the southern front, other operations occurred to the north and east. In early 1814, General Jackson had recruited another army that marched south toward the Creek stronghold at Tohopeka, or the Horseshoe, on the Tallapoosa. Before reaching his goal, the Red Sticks attacked at Emuckfau Creek (twice on 22 January 1814) and, during his subsequent retreat, again at Enitachopco village on 24 January 1814. The beaten Tennesseans returned to Fort Strother and Jackson again saw his militia dissolved as they were mustered out of the service. Simultaneous to these actions, General Floyd again led his Georgians toward the Red Stick town on the lower Tallapoosa River, where he was attacked and defeated in the Battle of Calebee Creek (27 January 1814) and was compelled to retreat.

The decisive blow in the war was finally struck by General Jackson's third army, which this time successfully reached the Creek stronghold at Tohopeka and severely defeated the Red Sticks on 27 March 1814. Heeding rumors that the Creeks would attempt one final stand at the Hickory Ground, near the confluence of the Coosa and Tallapoosa rivers, Jackson coordinated his army's movements with the advance of Brigadier General Joseph Graham's Carolina Brigade and Colonel Homer Milton's unit of the Third Regiment. When these elements arrived at Fort Jackson, located at the confluence of the Coosa and Tallapoosa rivers, Jackson learned that many hostile Creeks had evaded their pursuers and were on the way to Pensacola and Spanish Florida. However, it soon became evident that the Creek War was virtually ended, as thousands of starving, defeated Indians began to gather at the forts of the conquering white armies. Throughout the spring and summer of 1814, Indians continued to surrender at forts, some of their own will and others when captured by American troops.

Military forces were concentrated at Fort Jackson. One operation in the Upper Alabama River Valley that was directed from this post was that of Colonel Pearson and a detachment of Carolina troops that searched the upper valley region during May and June. On 24 May, the 39th Regiment U.S. Infantry, commanded by Colonel Thomas Hart Benton, left Fort Jackson for Fort Claiborne. On this movement General Graham commented:

> The 39th U.S. Infantry 600 in number left this place in boats and descended the Alabama for the Heights: I endeavored to impress on Colonel Benton who [is] commanded to land parties and scour such part of the country as Colonel Pearson would not by reason of its extent. (Graham to General Pinckney, 24 May 1814, Letterbook, Graham Papers)

Colonel Milton was also sent down river to join the remainder of the Third Regiment under Russell. Thus, for a time, Fort Claiborne became the headquarters of the regular army with responsibility for dispersing concentrations of hostile Indians along the Florida line (Doster, 1974: 2:103).

While the Creek War campaigns had thus far been directed solely against the hostile Creeks, the changing course of the war with Britain now led Jackson and others to consider the possibility of a British invasion of the Gulf Coast. The importance of controlling the Alabama River and its tributaries was appreciated by both the Americans and the British. Admiral Cochrane, commander of the British invasion fleet, originally planned to capture Mobile and then, using flatboats mounted with naval guns, move inland to the Creek country, destroying the American forts guarding the route (Owsley, 1981). Because it was feared that the remaining bands of hostile Red Sticks might regroup, be resupplied by the Spanish or British at Pensacola, and renew their attacks, the Alabama River forts were designed to serve a double purpose—to withstand any British attack and to function as supply points and bases of operations against any future Indian or British threat (Joseph Graham Papers, Letterbook, 17 May 1814).

By fall, Major General Jackson had returned to negotiate a peace treaty with the Creeks. In the Treaty of Fort Jackson, signed on 9 August 1814, the Creeks ceded twenty million acres of land including all of their territory west of the Coosa and south of a line running from just north of Fort Jackson east and then southeastward to the Chattahoochee River. In this treaty, Jackson deliberately attempted to isolate the main body of Creeks from Spanish Florida and thus seize the entire Alabama River Valley. Within a few days of the treaty, Jackson and the 44th Regiment U.S. Infantry descended the Alabama River to prepare for the defense of the Gulf Coast against the British. However, the Treaty of Ghent formally ended hostilities between Great Britain and the United States soon after the Battle of New Orleans in January 1815.

Summary

The Creek War of 1813-1814 greatly reduced the political and military importance of the Creeks. By the end of that war, the Indians also lost a significant portion of their traditional lands. In the ensuing years, increased pressure for cession of the remaining Creek territory came from both the state governments of Alabama and Georgia and the federal government. A second Creek War was brief; by 1836 forced Indian removal was a reality, and with its end also came a termination of the Creeks as a nation in Alabama.

Archaeologists at Auburn University have recently taken an active role in anthropological research of the Creek Indians. These investigations have combined both archaeological and ethnohistorical approaches to a more complete understanding of the history of the Creek Indians in central and eastern Alabama. To date, significant information has been gathered from archaeological surveys along the Tallapoosa, Coosa, and Chattahoochee river valleys. Actual excavations have been conducted on the site of Fort Jackson in Elmore County and at a mid-eighteenth-century Creek village in Lee County. Most recently, extensive excavations have been conducted at the large town of Hoithlewaulee, located along the Tallapoosa River in Elmore County. All of these endeavors have provided basic knowledge crucial for an understanding of Creek cultural history, and especially a better understanding of the direction and mechanisms of Upper Creek cultural change—such as those associated with the first Creek War.

Bibliography

Austill, Jere
  1923   "Reminiscences of Jere Austill." *Arrow Points* 6:23-32.

Boyd, Mark F.
  1937   "Events at Prospect Bluff on the Apalachicola River, 1808-1818." *Florida Historical Quarterly* 16:55-96.

Claiborne, John Francis Hamtramck
  1880   *Mississippi as a province, territory and state with biographical notices of eminent citizens.* Jackson MS: Power and Barksdale.

Cooke, Leonard Calvert
  1935   "The development of the road system of Alabama." M.A. thesis, University of Alabama.

Cotterill, Robert Spencer
  1954   *The Southern Indians: the story of the civilized tribes before removal.* Norman: University of Oklahoma Press.

Doster, James F.
  1974   *Creek Indians: the Creek Indians and their Florida Lands, 1740-1823.* New York: Garland Publishing, Inc., 2 volumes.

Graham, Joseph
  1814   Joseph Graham Papers, Correspondence, Letterbook, General Orders and Orderly Books. Original at North Carolina Department of Cultural Resources, Division of Archives and History.

Halbert, H. S. and T. H. Ball
  1969   *The Creek War of 1813 and 1814.* Edited, with introduction and notes by Frank L. Owsley, Jr., University AL: University of Alabama Press.

Hamilton, Peter J.
  1898   "Early roads of Alabama." *Transactions of the Alabama Historical Society,* 1897-1898, volume 2.

Hamilton, Peter J. and Thomas M. Owen

    1898   "Topographical notes and observations on the Alabama River, August 1814, by Major Howell Tatum." *Transactions of the Alabama Historical Society,* 1897-1898, volume 2.

Harris, W. Stuart

    1977   *Dead towns of Alabama.* University AL: University of Alabama Press.

Lowrie, Walter and Matthew St. Clair Clarke, eds.

    1832   *American State Papers.* Documents, legislative and executive, of the Congress of the United States, from the first session of the first to the third session of the thirteenth Congress, inclusive: commencing 3 March 1789 and ending 3 March 1815. Volume 4, Washington: Gales and Seaton.

Mooney, James

    1965   *The Ghost-Dance Religion and the Sioux Outbreak of 1890.* Chicago: University of Chicago Press.

Nunez, Theron A., Jr.

    1958   "Creek nativism and the Creek War of 1813-1814." *Ethnohistory* 5:1-47, 131-75, 292-301.

Owen, Thomas M.

    1911   "Alabama roads and highways: an historical introduction." *Bulletin* no. 2, State Highway Department.

Owsley, Frank Lawrence, Jr.

    1981   *Struggle for the Gulf borderlands, the Creek War and the Battle of New Orleans, 1812-1815.* Gainesville: University Presses of Florida.

Pickett, Albert James

    1962   *History of Alabama and incidentally of Georgia and Mississippi, from the earliest period.* Birmingham AL: Birmingham Book and Magazine Co.

Pound, Merritt Bloodworth

    1951   *Benjamin Hawkins, Indian Agent.* Athens: University of Georgia Press.

Prucha, Francis Paul

    1962   *American Indian policy in the formative years: the Indian trade and Intercourse acts, 1790-1834*. Lincoln: University of Nebraska Press.

Sheehan, Bernard W.

    1973   *Seeds of extinction: Jeffersonian Philanthropy and the American Indian*. New York: W. W. Norton & Company.

Wallace, Anthony F. C.

    1956   "Revitalization movements: Some theoretical considerations for their comparative study." *American Anthropologist* 58:264-81.

    1972   *The death and rebirth of the Seneca*. New York: Vintage Books.

Telling Observations:

Early Travelers

in East-Central Alabama

Walter Bertram Hitchcock, Jr.

The first literary impressions of Alabama were recorded by those hardy travelers of the late eighteenth century and the first half of the nineteenth century who came to this raw country to prepare eyewitness reports for their more civilized readers. These first-person narratives of overland journeys and encounters with pioneers of various colors and trades were excellent journalism in their own time. Today, the accounts, taken together, constitute a body of literature prophetic in nature. As Bert Hitchcock shows in this closely focused study of the last wave of early travel literature, the sojourners were more than snobbish or superficial observers. They had a sharp eye for the particular and many were able to see the general paradox of Alabama's statehood—that contrast between awesome natural promise and a populace that could not measure up to it. Modern Alabamians, pondering who we are and casting back for answers to this, the most perplexing of historical questions, will find something more than physical descriptions in this travel literature. The people who first settled this state gave to the place a tone and a character that has not changed greatly in two hundred years. Hitchcock helps us to see these historical continuities and to view Alabama as more than a geographical abstraction. He brings to this study his own wide reading and Alabama experience. With graduate training at the University of Melbourne, the University of Oregon and Duke University, he has a special interest in writing about Alabama. He is a native of Demopolis. In addition to his duties as head of Auburn University's English department, he is now preparing an encyclopedic reference book on the state's literature.

DURING THE FIRST FIVE DECADES of the nineteenth century, many travelers, both American and European, journeyed through east-central Alabama. A number of them did not just travel, however: they published accounts of their experiences. As a result, a wealth of travel literature exists about this area.

To enhance the discussion of these writings, it would be helpful to say a word or two about *why* these people came here. The explanation is found in three words: we were "on the route" or "on *the* route." For a number of years, east-central Alabama was a particularly fascinating portion of the territory lying along a major thoroughfare to the lower American west, a route that became a main artery of emigration to the great beckoning frontier and, in time, a leg of the standard, almost obligatory, southern and western "tour" undertaken by visitors to the United States.

The third, fourth, and fifth decades of the nineteenth century were the heyday of literate European, especially British, travelers in America. The United States, having vindicated itself yet again in the War of 1812, became an object of intense trans-Atlantic curiosity. Our great experiment in Jacksonian democracy was underway, and inextricably tied to the destiny of white America were the dual processes—now to be seen in all their fascinating vividness—of the mass displacement of the American Indian and the solidifying of our system of enslavement of blacks. Just as the territory where we now live was once initially the center of the British-French-Spanish struggle to possess the continent, so then it became a focal point again; it was a locale in which the past, present, and future of the United States could be seen, where important primary evidence might be gained by which to speculate upon the ultimate success or the impending doom of the American republic. The world was curious, the U.S. itself was anxious about world opinion, and a host of hearty journal-keepers and perceptive publishers did not fail to recognize opportunity when it was presented to them.

During the eighteenth century, the old Indian trails between major Creek villages, especially those trails running west and southwest through this territory to the marvelous inland rivers— the Coosa, Tallapoosa, and Alabama—became standard trading paths for Englishmen traveling from Charleston and other points east. The section through our area was what William Bartram referred to as the "Southern Trail," or "The Great Trading Path." In 1805 "trail" and "path" gave way to something of greater appellation. What was officially and properly called "a horse path" originally, and later Three Notch Road (because of the triple blazing used), soon became known gloriously as the Federal Road. The Creeks had demurred at an 1804 proposal to open a public way through their nation, but increased pressure from Washington pushed them into assent late the following year. Article II of the Convention of Washington of 14 November 1805 read:

> It is hereby stipulated and agreed, on the part of the Creek nation, that the government of the United States shall forever hereafter have a right to a horse path, through the Creek Country, from the Ocmulgee to the Mobile, in such direction as shall, by the President of the United States, be considered most convenient, and to clear out the same, and lay logs over the creeks: And the citizens of said States, shall at all times have a right to pass peaceably on said path, under such regulations and restrictions, as the government of the United States shall from time to time direct; and the Creek chiefs will have boats kept at the several rivers for the conveyance of men and horses, and houses of entertainment established at suitable places on said path for the accommodation of travellers; and the respective ferriages and prices of entertainment for men and horses, shall be regulated by the present agent, Colonel Haw-

kins, or by his successor in office, or as is usual among white people.

A foot in the door, a hoof on the path, was all that was needed, of course. In April of 1806 Congress appropriated $6,400 for its new route, then $5,000 more in 1809. In 1811 additional permission was secured to widen the path, and federal troops were assigned to do the work. Regular appropriations followed—$5,000 in 1816, $5,000 in 1818, $3,300 in 1820, and $6,000 in 1826. A Congressional Act of 10 February 1833 authorized the opening of a new post road through this country and appropriated $20,000 for it as well as several thousand for much-needed repair of the old road, which had to continue in use during construction of the new. By the mid-1830s three separate stage lines—the Mail Line, the Telegraph Line, and the People's Line—were operating on this route between Columbus and Montgomery.

Generally following the "Lower Creek Trading Path," the Federal Road did not go to the extensive Indian settlements on the lower Tallapoosa River. Instead it veered southwest from a point east of Montgomery in order to intersect with a second famous Indian trail, the Pensacola and Mobile Path. An integral part of the history of our area, the old Federal Road might be called the pathway that led to Alabama's statehood.

Since it will be important for a few of our travelers, let me mention also the road that was the successor of the Federal Road—the railroad. The Montgomery Railroad Company was chartered in 1834 to construct a line from Montgomery to the Chattahoochee River—88.5 miles; it was the second railroad in Alabama. That the track was built west to east says a great deal about the settlement of east and central Alabama since 1805. Still, the undertaking was not without numerous difficulties, not the least of which was financial. Construction progress was slow until the late 1830s when state aid was finally secured and added to the monies of private enterprise. By 1840, 33.5 miles were open for travel, and by 1847, another 60 miles—from Montgomery to Auburn. Not until April of 1851, over seventeen years after it was chartered, did the Montgomery-West Point railroad reach its eastern terminus. The cost, according to an 1854 report, was $1,113,345.98.

Understanding the background of the whys and hows of early nineteenth-century journeys through east Alabama, we can now sample some of the fruits of such travel. Let's look first at the descriptions of *the land*, the natural environment, followed by observations of *the people*, the human beings—red, black, and white—who were encountered by these travelers. Finally, let me attempt to meaningfully combine the two, considering first some accounts of the great vicissitudes of travel through the area, and then some larger articulated conclusions that were the thoughtful result of personal experience with a new country and its people.

The Land. The land of east Alabama, whenever it was possible to see it in its pristine state, was pleasingly impressive to travelers. As had some of the Spaniards earlier, James Adair, an Irishman who journeyed among the Creeks in the eighteenth century, remarked on the "large beautiful" streams along which the Indians lived, "where the lands are fertile, the water clean and well tasted, and the air extremely pure." As the decades passed, it was necessary, of course, to go increasingly farther west to find a large expanse of such territory. Nonetheless, much natural beauty remained.

According to some nineteenth-century reports, the scenery was unparalleled, the beauty supreme. Even acknowledging the exaggerated romantic, and nationalistic, impulses in a piece called "Notes of a Southern Excursion" that was included in Caroline Gilman's *The Poetry of Travelling in the United States* (1838), we still cannot fail to be impressed. Gazing west from the banks of the Chattahoochee River near Columbus into the very eastern edge of our territory, a person was presented "one of the most magnificent displays of scenery which Nature or Art had ever presented. . . ." "All that the mind can conceive of beauty is here depicted in the sight of the setting sun, on a calm lovely evening in summer." Here again was "Eden," an "earthly paradise." The beauty of this place, the writer contended, cannot be lost "in comparison with any spot on earth":

> The scenery of the Hudson has been extolled as being the most sublime and picturesque to be found in the wide-extended continent of America, and comparable to the most beautiful specimens even on the banks of the Rhine. But I doubt not, however, that in

many of the wilder and less frequented portions of the States, there may be found scenery, which, if but seen as often by persons of taste, and panegyrised by as able pens, would rival the far-famed Hudson. A day's ramble on the river Chatahouchie has confirmed me in the above opinion, and I am convinced, that to one of a poetic fancy, no place is better calculated to call forth those high and ec-static feelings which none but poets know, than a visit to its wild and uncultivated banks. Not only has Nature, with an unsparing hand, been lavish to this spot, in elevating the towering hill, in-serting the craggy rock, and placing the bold and beautiful river to meander beneath them; but here is also to be seen the flowery vale, interspersed with numerous specimens from Flora's hand. Speci-mens of unparalleled beauty overhang the mossy banks of the river, and skirt the brow of the rugged bluff. While, waving over them in monarch-like majesty, the elegant magnolia, shadowy oak, and loftier and more desolate pine, seem to protect them from the blasts of the hurricane, and promise succor and shelter from the ever-returning frosts of October.

Actually antecedent to, but what can appear now as echoes of, this particular panegyric comes from other non-American and non-romantic travelers. David Taitt, an agent of the British government on a mission in the interior of Alabama in 1772, observed quite dif-ferent natural scenes. To him, too, however, the effect was still one of beauty, such beauty that it seemed "more like the works of Art than of Nature." And A. Levasseur, who was General LaFayette's secretary during his tour of America in 1824-1825 and who crossed the Chattahoochee River only a few miles south of where Gilman's observer had been, wrote: "the country around was so beautiful, that it yet appears to me as the most beautiful spot I ever visited."

To be sure, the natural wildness of the country called forth other characterizations. Lorenzo Dow, the famous eccentric itinerant preacher who came through the Alabama Creek territory in 1805, wrote of his overnight stays here as ones in a "desert, inhabited only by wild beasts, whilst the wolves were howling on every side." Thirty years later some of the wilderness and some of the wolves were still here. To J. Marion Sims, a young South Carolinian going out on a doctor's night call near Mt. Meigs in 1836, the cold and the dark of this "wild" country, with wolves "howling in every direction," made the scene "a very novel one indeed."

There are numerous specific descriptions of the natural environment that offer greater appreciation and gratitude than we find in Dow and Sims. Especially is this true in earlier accounts. To London *Times* correspondent William Howard Russell, who made the trip in 1861, the land of east Alabama was "more undulating, and somewhat more picturesque, or less unattractive" than the west Georgia countryside through which he had passed. On the whole, however, he found that it had "little to recommend it, except the natural fertility of the soil." Frederick Law Olmsted, the great American landscape architect, traveled through here in the 1850s, and his reaction was similar. From Columbus to Montgomery he traveled by rail through what was for him an unexceptional "hilly wilderness." Had Olmsted been an earlier traveler, however, he doubtlessly would have experienced in east Alabama what now he had to go to central Alabama to see. Struck with awe, he described standing atop Goat Hill in Montgomery and viewing in every direction "a dense forest, boundless as the sea, and producing in the mind the same solemn sensation."

Similar sensations had been provoked by the scenery of east Alabama in preceding years. Unlike William Howard Russell, Englishman James S. Buckingham found in 1839 a significant difference between the land in Alabama and that in Georgia. The "change of aspect in scenery and condition was very striking," he wrote. Coming into Alabama he found that "the woods . . . seemed more wild . . . , the land . . . more undulated in surface, the swamps in the bottoms . . . more abundant; [and] the brooks ran with greater impetuosity." As he proceeded westward, according to Buckingham, the soil became richer, and "the woods were much more variegated, as, besides the ever-succeeding pine, there was a thick underwood of various flowering shrubs and trees, including magnolias, yellow jessamines, the dogwood, and the grape-vine, with a very beautiful tree called the willow-oak."

Traveling south rather than east through some of the same territory in 1791, John Pope of Virginia also remarked on the floral variety, despite what he said was "the natural sterility" of the soil. Here, he wrote, "long-leaf'd pine, hickory, oak, poplar, and walnut trees grow . . . and protect from the scorching . . . sun the tall and tender grass, among which plants, shrubs, and flowers of variegated hue, and of rare medicinal virtues, are interspersed." Even in regions of sandy soil, George William Featherstonhaugh, an English geographer, reported in the mid 1830s that laurels, live oaks, and other evergreens grew thickly along the banks of streams that ran "pleasantly at the base of graceful pine hills . . . and wild grass was growing every where in great profusion." Tyrone Power, the Irish actor who passed through Alabama in 1834-1835, reported traveling for nine straight hours "through a forest of pine growing out of a sandy soil, without any undergrowth whatever,—the trees of the noblest height, and just so far apart that horsemen might have galloped in any direction without difficulty." To British writer Thomas Hamilton in 1831 travel here was through "one continued pine forest." But to James Stuart, a Scottish newspaperman, a great deal of natural variety presented itself in his travel through east Alabama in March of 1830, and he commented at appropriate length. Like James Buckingham, Stuart found the beauty of Alabama "greatly increased" from that of Georgia, especially "as respects trees and evergreens." Stuart made his way through a forest composed of underwood interspersed with a few great forest trees that had vines growing to their very top. Some of the groves seemed to have been "formed by art." There were, he reported, "many splendid oaks, tulip-trees, chesnuts and sycamores, skirting the woods." Here, too, were magnolias "in great numbers, dog-wood, . . . and the red-bud . . . of great size, covered with a profusion of the most beautiful colours." But nothing, Stuart concluded, "is more beautiful in the woods than the dog-wood."

This opinion about the dogwood had already been voiced by naturalist William Bartram. But Stuart's general description and feelings were affectingly reproduced by the famous English female traveler Harriet Martineau, who passed through Alabama's Creek country in April of 1835 and who added another candidate for floral supremacy:

> The woods were superb in their spring beauty. The thickets were in full leaf; and the ground was gay with violets, may-apple, buck-eye, blue lupin, iris, and crow-poison. The last is like the

white lily, growing close to the ground. Its root, boiled, mixed with corn, and thrown out into the fields, poisons crows. If eaten by cattle, it injures but does not destroy them. The sour-wood is a beautiful shrub. To-day it looked like a splendid white fuchsia, with tassels of black butterflies hanging from the extremities of the twigs. But the grandest flower of all, perhaps the most exquisite I ever beheld, is the honeysuckle of the southern woods. It bears little resemblance to the ragged flower which has the same name elsewhere. It is a globe of blossoms, larger than my hand, growing firmly at the end of an upright stalk, with the richest and most harmonious colouring, the most delicate long anthers, and the flowers exquisitely grouped among the leaves. It is the queen of flowers. I generally contrived, in my journeys through the southern States, to have a bunch of honeysuckles in the stage before my eyes; and they seemed to be visible wherever I turned, springing from the roots of the forest trees, or dangling from their topmost boughs, or mixing in with the various greens of the thickets.

Let me conclude this look at the land with the reports of two professionals—one an eighteenth- and one a nineteenth-century natural scientist. Sir Charles Lyell, the eminent British geologist, made a fifty-five mile journey by stage westward from Columbus in 1846. He passed

through an undulating country, sometimes on the tertiary sands covered with pines, sometimes in swamps enlivened by green palmetto and tall magnolia, and occasionally crossing into the borders of the granitic region, where there appeared immediately a mixture of oak, hickory, and pine. There was no grass growing under the pine trees, and the surface of the ground was every where strewed with yellow leaves, and the fallen needles of the fir trees. The sound of the wind in the boughs of the long-leaved pines always reminded me of the waves breaking on a distant sea-shore, and it was agreeable to hear it swelling gradually, and then dying away, as the breeze rose and fell.

Sir Charles also had an interest in history that complemented his scientific bent. Observing a great many pine or fir stumps in a new clearing where he left the stage to board the train for Montgomery, he became curious, he says, "to know how many years it would take to restore such a forest if once destroyed":

The first stump I examined measured two feet five inches in diameter at the height of three feet from the ground, and I counted in it 120 rings of annual growth; a second measured less by two inches in diameter, yet was 260 years old; a third, at the height of two feet above the ground, although 180 years old, was only two feet in diameter; a fourth, the oldest I could find, measured, at the height of three feet above its base, four feet, and presented 320 rings of annual growth; and I could have counted a few more had the tree been cut down even with the soil. The height of these trees varied 70 to 120 feet. From the time taken to acquire the above dimensions, we may confidently infer that no such trees will be seen by posterity, after the clearing of the country, except where they may happen to be protected for ornamental purposes.

Sixty-eight years earlier, William Bartram had seen these trees in their glory. In 1777-1778, he reported that in the Alabama Creek country there were grand high forests of majestic trees and expansive natural grassy plains, or savannas. Bartram was impressed with the large and stately trees often hung with wild grapes, but he was no less impressed with what he described as a "remarkable grove" of dogwood trees he once traveled through. These beautiful dogwoods, twelve feet high, with an occasional magnolia among them, continued "nine or ten miles unalterable." Their branches, "spreading horizontally" and "meeting and interlocking with each other, formed one vast, shady, cool grove, so dense and humid as to exclude the sun-beams, and prevent the intrusion of almost every other vegetable. . . ." Bartram, a botanist, found delight in the topography and flora of east Alabama. In his travels here he viewed, as those who followed him could not, "a magnificent and pleasing sylvan landscape of primitive, uncultivated nature."

What came to change this magnificent landscape was, of course, people—not its original inhabitants, not mere travelers, but the numerous settlers. This was frontier country and the early settlers were self-seeking, frontier people.

The People. The "licentious behavior" of the traders who came into the Creek territory evoked extensive comment by Englishman David Taitt in the eighteenth century. Most of these adventurers, he said, were deserters, horse-thieves, and other unsavory types.

General LaFayette's secretary, Monsieur Levasseur, echoed Taitt's view after traveling through east Alabama in 1825:

> We passed the night on the banks of Line Creek, in a small village of the same name, almost entirely inhabited by persons whom the love of gain had assembled from all parts of the globe, in the midst of these deserts, to turn to their own profit the simplicity and above all the new wants of the unfortunate natives. These avaricious wretches, who without scruple poison the tribes with intoxicating liquors, and afterwards ruin them by duplicity and overreaching, are the most cruel and dangerous enemies of the Indian nation, whom at the same time they accuse of being robbers, idlers, and drunkards. If the limits to which I had determined to restrain my narrative had not been overstepped, I would easily show, that these vices with which they reproach the children of the forest, are the result of the approach of civilization, and also in how many instances they are surpassed by the whites in cruelty and want of faith.

The Indians. Two British travelers, one in 1828 and another in 1831, had the opportunity to view the Creeks in the more natural context of one of their great ball-playing occasions. The first, Captain Basil Hall, was struck most by the ceremonial preparations by team members, which included making hundreds of cuts on their bodies by means of gar teeth set in corn cobs. "I scarcely knew how to feel when I found myself amongst some dozens of naked savages, streaming with blood from top to toe, skipping and yelling round a fire, or talking at the top of their voices in a language of which I knew nothing, or laughing as merrily as if it were the best fun in the world to be cut to pieces." But consternation changed to admiration when Hall saw these warriors just before the game. They provided "some of the finest specimens of the human form I have ever beheld." Whether they were stretched out on the grass, leaning against a tree, or just standing with their arms folded, "all of them unconsciously fell into attitudes of such perfect ease and gracefulness, as would have enchanted the heart of a painter."

Thomas Hamilton was similarly impressed at a Creek-Ewitche ball game that he witnessed:

> The players on each side soon appeared, and retired to the neighbouring thickets to adjust their toilet for the game. While thus en-

gaged, either party endeavoured to daunt their opponents by loud and discordant cries. At length they emerged with their bodies entirely naked except the waist, which was encircled by a girdle. Their skin was besmeared with oil, and painted fantastically with different colours. Some wore tails, others necklaces made of the teeth of animals, and the object evidently was to look as ferocious as possible. After a good deal of preliminary ceremony, the game began. . . .

I certainly never saw a finer display of agile movement. In figure the Creek Indians are tall and graceful. There is less volume of muscle than in Englishmen, but more activity and freedom of motion. Many of the players were handsome men, and one in particular might have stood as the model of an Apollo. His form and motions displayed more of the *ideal* than I had ever seen actually realized in a human figure. . . .

At length the Creeks were victorious, and the air rang with savage shouts of triumph. . . . The victors danced about in all the madness of inordinate elation, and the evening terminated in a profuse jollification, to which I had the honour of contributing.

James Stuart was also impressed with the Creeks he saw in 1830. They were well mounted "and very handsomely dressed in their own fashion. Their scarlet turbans, their blue dress covered with beads, and their long spurs gave them an imposing appearance . . . when their accoutrements were not too nearly inspected."

Unfortunately, sad, pathetic pictures of the Indians grew to outnumber the positive, admiring ones. Tyrone Power reported the "extreme wretchedness" of the condition of most of the Creeks late in 1834. A kettle seemed to be the only "furniture" many of them owned and their "wigwams" of bark or green boughs were "of the frailest and most uncomfortable construction." Some of the Creek chiefs were men of wealth, but John Pope gives an unforgettable picture of one who had early succumbed to the influence of the white man: "It is said *Black Dog* is a man of property, tho' a most egregious sot and sluggard. —I once saw his Majesty in a puddle of his own excrement and urine, which attracted swarms of *Spanish Flies* and *Beetles*, whose constant buzz had lull'd him into sweet repose."

G. W. Featherstonhaugh was as informative if slightly less graphic in his descriptions from 1835:

> Everything as we advanced into the Creek country announced the total dissolution of order. Indians of all ages were wandering about listlessly, the poorest of them having taken to begging, and when we came in sight would come and importune us for money. Some of them, imitating the whites, were doing their best to prey upon each other, for we frequently saw squaws belonging to some of the chiefs seated by the roadside at a log or rude table with a bottle of whiskey, and a glass to supply their unfortunate countrymen who had anything to give in return, even if it were only the skin of an animal. . . . In other places we met young men in the flower of their age, dressed in ragged hunting shirts and turbans, staggering along, and often falling to the ground, with empty bottles in their hands: in this wretched state of things, with the game almost entirely destroyed, it is evident that nothing will soon be left to those who have beggared themselves but to die of want, or to emigrate, a step they are so very averse to take that in their desperation they have already committed some murders. . . . No language can describe the filth inside of [the Indian cabins] . . . and the disgusting appearance of their tenants, especially the old crones. . . . [One] was an old creature turned sixty, the most thoroughly hideous, wrinkled, dark, and dirty hag I have even seen amongst them. . . . [She] was completely stark naked.

The Blacks. Because this race was literally caught between the Indians and the whites, it is appropriate to consider them in that position here. Most of the black slaves observed by our travelers were in transit themselves, but a transit far less pleasant than that of their paying-traveler observers. Harriet Martineau wrote:

> We saw to-day, the common sight of companies of slaves travelling westwards; and the very uncommon one of a party returning into South Carolina. When we overtook such a company proceeding westwards, and asked where they were going, the answer commonly given by the slaves was, "Into Yellibama."—Sometimes these poor creatures were encamped, under the care of the slave-trader, on the banks of a clear stream, to spend a day in washing their clothes. Sometimes they were loitering along the road; the old folks and infants mounted on the top of a wagon-load of luggage;

the ablebodied, on foot, perhaps silent, perhaps laughing; the prettier of the girls, perhaps with a flower in the hair, and a lover's arm around her shoulder. There were wide differences in the air and gait of these people. It is usual to call the most depressed of them brutish in appearance. In some sense they are so; but I never saw in any brute an expression of countenance so low, so lost, as the most degraded class of negroes. There is some life and intelligence in the countenance of every animal; even in that of "the silly sheep," nothing so dead as the vacant, unheeding look of the depressed slave is to be seen. To-day there was a spectacle by the roadside which showed that this has nothing to do with negro nature. . . . To-day, we passed, in the Creek Territory, an establishment of Indians who held slaves. Negroes are anxious to be sold to Indians, who give them moderate work, and accommodations as good as their own. Those seen today among the Indians, were sleek, intelligent, and cheerful-looking, like the most favored house-slaves, or free servants of colour, where the prejudice is least strong.

Thomas Hamilton confirms Martineau's recognition of the comparatively different cast of black slavery under the Indians, but more travelers noted the plight of slaves under white owners. Featherstonhaugh also noted the groups in transit:

In the course of the day we met a great many families of planters emigrating to Alabama and Mississippi to take up cotton plantations, their slaves tramping through the waxy ground on foot, and the heavy wagons containing the black women and children slowly dragging on, and frequently breaking down. All that were able were obliged to walk, and being wet with fording the streams were shivering with cold. The negroes suffer very much in these expeditions conducted in the winter season, and upon this occasion must have been constantly wet, for I am sure we forded forty to fifty streams this day, which, although insignificant in dry weather, were at this time very much swollen with rain. We passed at least 1000 negro slaves, all trudging on foot, and worn down with fatigue.

Conditions, if different, did not seem to be much better when the slaves reached their plantation destination, according to James Buckingham. While his coach was under repair, "we had an opportunity of seeing the great bulk of the labourers on the [neighboring] plantation. These were all negro slaves; . . . the few garments they had being almost wholly in rags, and their persons and apparel so filthy, that it might be doubted whether either the one or the other were ever washed from one end of the year to the other."

Sir Charles Lyell reported from his 1846 junket through Alabama that "I witnessed no mal-treatment of slaves in this State, but drunkenness prevails to such a degree among their owners, that I can not doubt that the power they exercise must often be fearfully abused."

The Whites. The point of entry into Alabama for most of our travelers was across the Chattahoochee from Columbus. What an entry it was! Basil Hall saw the city in 1828 in its beginnings—a trailer city, houses on wheels ready to make the fast move into the territory across the river. "During the short period we were there," he reported, "many new comers dropped in from different directions, out of the forest—like birds of prey attracted by the scent of some glorious quarry." Seven years later Harriet Martineau noted a great many gentlemanly individuals in the streets of Columbus and wrote that "it bears the appearance of being a thriving, spacious, handsome village, well worth stopping to see." Hers was definitely a minority opinion.

There may have been natural beauty to be experienced at or near Columbus, but most visitors saw little human beauty in it. Upon arriving in Columbus, James Buckingham declared that "we thought that we had . . . arrived at the *ne plus ultra* of disorder, neglect, and dirtiness; though we were told, in the ordinary phrase, that we might 'go farther and fare worse.' " Just across the river was a little farther and in many ways a lot worse. Here, later to be called Girard and, later still, Phenix City, was a village that was first given the appropriate name of Sodom. In 1834, it was, according to Tyrone Power, "a wild-looking village," "its denizens composed chiefly of 'minions o' the moon,' outlaws from the neighboring states . . . gamblers and other desperate men." Every so often these "bold outlaws" would go over en masse for an evening's frolic in Columbus, as the U.S. Marshal stood by, or hid, helplessly. In Sodom, George Featherstonhaugh reported that he "found the lowest stage of drunkenness and debauchery," although the main street of Columbus itself swarmed with drunks and prostitutes. Things seemed to have gotten worse before they got better. Olmsted wrote from his experience of the mid-1850s: "I had seen in no place, since I left Washington, so much gambling, intoxication, and cruel treatment of servants in public, as in Columbus. . . . I must caution persons, travelling for health or pleasure, to avoid stopping in the town." It is best, Olmsted went on, for a person going west from Savannah not to spend the night anywhere between Macon and Montgomery!

Several travelers testify specifically to the clear increase of drinking, swearing, and tobacco chewing as they moved westward across Alabama. Columbus provided a fair introduction to the violence they would also increasingly witness. In addition to the great amounts of liquor for sale everywhere in Columbus, James Buckingham was surprised at "the open sale of dirks, bowie knives, and . . . 'Arkansas toothpick[s].' " These items were sold by druggists as a matter of course—"plainly indicating, that weapons to kill, as well as medicine to cure, could be had at the same shop; and placing beside the deadly poisons of arsenic, laudanum, hemlock, and hellbore, the deadly weapons of no less fatal power." Alexis de Tocqueville, probably the most perceptive foreign observer the United States has ever had, recorded a conversation he had with a lawyer in Montgomery in January of 1832:

> Is it then true that the ways of the people of Alabama are as violent as is said?
>
> Yes. There is no one here but carries arms under his clothes. At the slightest quarrel, knife or pistol comes to hand. These things happen continually; it is a semi-barbarous state of society.
>
> Q. But when a man is killed like that, is his assassin not punished?
>
> A. He is always brought to trial, and always acquitted by the jury, unless there are greatly aggravating circumstances. I cannot remember seeing a single man who was a little known pay with his life for such a crime. This violence has become accepted. . . . I have been no better myself than another in my time; look at the scars that cover my head (we did see the marks of four or five deep cuts). Those are knife blows I have been given.

Q. But you went to law?
A. My God! No. I tried to give as good in return.

The planter class of Alabama, whom we have tended to endow with attributes of high civilization, presented itself with no great favor to some visitors. James Buckingham gives us a specific description, Frederick Law Olmsted a generic one. Buckingham tells us (1839):

> Another of our passengers was a cotton planter, from the interior of Alabama, who was said to be worth 100,000 dollars, though his apparel certainly would not sell in any town of the United States for five dollars. He was about seventy years of age, had lost one eye, had only three or four teeth left, a sunburnt and wrinkled countenance, like parchment, with white locks hanging over his shoulders, a pair of scarlet cotton trousers, crossed with bars of deep blue, snuff-brown cotton stockings, shoes without buckles or strings, a short buttonless waistcoat, no braces, a nondescript coat, between a jacket and a surtout, no neckcloth, and a low-crowned and broad-brimmed brown hat. . . . When he learnt that we drank neither wine, beer, cider, or spirits, bathed or washed from head to foot once every day, took exercise for health, whether business required it or not, and never used tobacco in any form or shape, he said he felt less surprised than at first, at our health and vigour, but he thought it must require great resolution and perseverance to pursue so "singular a course of life," as he deemed this to be. . . . He said that he had never been in any church in all his life.

Frederick Law Olmsted's description from the 1850s reads:

> [The] cotton planters . . . were usually well-dressed, but were a rough, coarse style of people, drinking a great deal, and most of the time under a little alcoholic excitement. Not sociable, except when the topics of cotton, land, and negroes, were started; interested, however, in talk about theatres and the turf; very profane; often showing the handles of concealed weapons about their persons, but not quarrelsome, avoiding disputes and altercations, and respectful to one another in forms of words; very ill-informed, except on plantation business; their language very ungrammatical, idiomatic, and extravagant. Their grand characteristics—simplicity of motive, vague, shallow, and purely objective habits of thought; spontaneity and truthfulness of utterance, and bold, self-reliant

movement. . . . I was perplexed by finding, apparently united in the same individual, the self-possession and confidence of the well equipped gentleman, and the coarseness and low tastes of the un-civilized boor—frankness and reserve, recklessness and self re-straint, extravagance and penuriousness.

Among even the women and children of the lower classes were sights to cause consternation—for example, those reported by Sir Charles Lyell: a young mother smoking a pipe, a nine-year-old girl puffing on "paper cigars," and a baby being given tobacco to chew after being nursed at his mother's breast. Yet, even in what Buck-ingham called "a dissipated, gambling, idle, reckless, murdering population," some redeeming features could be found. Genuine ci-vility and gracious hospitality were gratefully noted, seeing a fron-tier family before the fire at their evening prayers was a moving experience, and pleasant indeed was the surprise of finding a book of Cowper's poems in a crude cabin which had "not even a pane of glass in the window."

That was the land and these the people—then. It was the land and its people combined that made the experience of travel. And traveling through east-central Alabama in the early nineteenth cen-tury was quite an experience. For Basil Hall, as for most of his fel-low travelers, finally getting to Montgomery and being able to take a steamboat was a welcome change after the fatiguing journey through the Creek country. At last, says Hall, "we had no chases after poultry,—no cooking to attend to—not so much extra com-pany to encumber us,—no fords or crazy bridges to cross, no four o'clock risings, or midnight travelling,—no broiling at noon, or freezing at night,—and lastly, but not least, no mosquitoes."

What often was traveled in east Alabama was, as James Stuart described it, "a mere track in the forest, in which many of the stumps of the trees still remain." There were stumps and fallen trees, an exciting if not always pleasant variety of wayside accom-modations, and usually, in great abundance, water and mud. But hear a few of the travelers directly—accounts unfavorable and favorable.

Thomas Hamilton distinctly remembered the roads of east-cen-tral Alabama (1831):

I have had occasion to say a great deal about roads in these volumes, but I pronounce that along which our route lay on the present occasion, to be positively, comparatively, and superlatively, the *very worst* I have ever travelled in the whole course of my peregrinations. The ruts were axle-deep, and huge crevices occasionally occurred, in which, but for great strategy on the part of the coachman, the vehicle would have been engulfed.

G. W. Featherstonhaugh also discovered the roads and roadside facilities to be memorable (1835):

> [The road] was so frightfully cut up as to render it impossible to sit in the vehicle: whenever it was dry enough, therefore, we walked, expecting every instant to see the carriage overturned. . . . At length we came to a low part of the country completely inundated, where it was impossible to walk, the water being in many places four feet deep. Here we are obliged to get in, and the old vehicle took to rolling in such a dreadful manner that every instant we expected to be soused into the water; and what rendered it really amusing was, that we were constantly obliged to draw up our limbs on the seat, for the water was at least eight inches deep in the bottom of the carriage, and went splashing about in the most extraordinary manner. All this time our trunks, which were lashed on behind, were being quietly dragged under the water. . . . We proceeded to one Macgirt'[s], a white man living in a filthy, Indian-looking place, who pretended to give us some breakfast, but it was so disgustingly bad that we were unable to touch it. This man said he expected every night to have his throat cut, which induced me to tell him, that if it would be any consolation, he might be quite sure they would not touch his victuals.

Both Harriet Martineau in 1835 and William Howard Russell in 1861 found hotel accommodations in Montgomery less than perfectly satisfactory. The place was filthy, Russell reported; "the feeding and the flies [were] intolerable." But "had it not been for the flies, the fleas would have been intolerable . . . [and so] one nuisance neutralized the other." Traveling to Montgomery, Russell had had to use his luggage for protection against the spitting of his fellow passengers aboard the train. Although the problem was renewed in his multi-occupancy hotel room, he was able finally to view the phenomenon with appreciative humor: "One of the gentlemen in the bed next the door was a tremendous projector in the tobacco juice line: his final rumination ere he sank to repose was a masterpiece of art—a perfect liquid pyrotechny, Roman candles and falling stars." Martineau arrived in Montgomery after a stagecoach trip through what one of her fellow passengers described as "the end of the world," a trip during which she had fallen into a creek. In her hotel room she did not find either water or sheets; she did find mice and "the dust of a twelvemonth" on the floor. The breakfast that was served the next morning was redemptive, however: tea, coffee, buns, cornbread, buckwheat cakes, broiled chicken, bacon, eggs, rice, hominy, fresh and pickled fish, and beefsteak.

For James Stuart, one particular Alabama meal was as comfortable and fine a one as "we found anywhere in travelling in the United States":

> We stopped at the hotel of Mrs. Lucas to dine. She has been a good-looking woman but now is fatter at her age (only thirty-five) than any woman I ever saw. . . . She takes the entire management of her house, and . . . manages it admirably. At dinner she sat at the head of the table, her husband sitting at one side; and the dinner, consisting of chicken-pie, ham, vegetables, pudding, and pie, was so neatly put upon the table, so well-cooked, and the dessert, consisting of dried fruits, preserved strawberries and plums, was so excellent, and withal the guests seemed to be made so welcome to every thing that was best, that Mrs. Lucas was, in our eyes, almost as meritorious a person as the old lady at the Bridge Inn, at Ferry-bridge in Yorkshire. . . . There was wine on the table, as well as brandy and water; and plenty of time was allowed us to partake of our repast. The whole charge was only three-quarters of a dollar for each person.

To conclude, I would like to share five of the more striking general opinions that emerged from various travelers' experiences in nineteenth-century Alabama. Observed George Featherston-haugh:

> Considering the softness of the climate here, and the great fertility of the soil in Alabama, it is not surprising that people should flock—as they do—to this favoured part of the United States. Still,

with all its advantages, I must say that I would rather be a visitor than a sojourner in the land: the persecuting malaria, which never pardons the country a single season, is of itself a great objection, and the universal and extravagant use of tobacco by the people would be to me another of equal magnitude; so, what with the effluvia of nature and man combined, this fine country, with all its advantages, seems to fall very far short of a terrestrial Paradise.

Looking about him at common Alabama dinner tables, Thomas Hamilton saw only "furrowed and haggard countenances" and was often moved to ask himself, "Is it possible that these men make pretension to happiness?" For Harriet Martineau, who was entertained in plantation homes, Alabama presented "an extreme case of the material advantages and moral evils of a new settlement." "The most prominent relief is the hospitality," she wrote, but the true state of the society is "false and hollow" because here "people forget that they must be just before they can be generous." "The wise will feel," she concludes, "that, though a man *may* save his soul anywhere, it is better to live on bread and water where existence is most idealized, than to grow suddenly rich in the gorgeous regions where mind is corrupted or starved amidst the luxuriance of nature."

One of the most moving vignettes in all of this travel literature appears in Tocqueville's *Democracy in America*; it is an account of his observation of an Indian woman, a negress, and a little white girl out in the woods. I will not give the full passage here, but only Tocqueville's closing:

> I had often chanced to see individuals met together in the same place, who belonged to the three races of men which people North America. I had perceived from many different results the preponderance of the Whites. But in the picture which I have just been describing there was something peculiarly touching; a bond of affection here united the oppressors with the oppressed, and the effort of Nature to bring them together rendered still more striking the immense distance placed between them by prejudice and by law.

For residents of Alabama today, the recognitions of James Silk Buckingham provide the most fitting and provocative of conclusions:

> Altogether the face of the country presented a combination of the grand, the useful, and the beautiful, which made it rank, in our estimation, as one of the finest we had ever traversed. Carrying the imagination forward in prospect, we could not but think that in less than a century hence, when population and capital, railroads and other improvements, shall have filled up this immense territory with its fair share of enjoyers in proportion to its means of enjoyment, it will equal, if not surpass, the very finest parts of England or France; and if well and wisely governed, be as happy a country, as it is sure to become a rich and productive one. Nature has done everything to make it so; and if it fails, it will be the fault of its institutions or its inhabitants.

Bibliography

Selected travel volumes, mainly accounts of eighteenth- and nineteenth-century journeys through east-central Alabama.

Bartram, William. *The Travels of William Bartram.* Edited by Mark Van Doren. New York: Facsimile Library, 1940.

Bourne, Edward Gaylord, ed. *Narratives of the Career of Hernando DeSoto.* New York: A. S. Barnes, 1904.

*Buckingham, James Silk. *The Slave States of America.* London: Fisher, Son, & Co., 1842.

Dow, Lorenzo. *The Life—Travels, Labors, and Writings, of Lorenzo Dow.* New York: R. Worthington, 1881.

*Featherstonhaugh, George W. *Excursion through the Slave States.* New York: Harper, 1844.

Gilman, Caroline Howard. *The Poetry of Travelling in the United States.* With additional sketches by a few friends; and "A Week Among Autographs," by Rev. S. Gilman. New York: S. Colman, 1838.

Hall, Basil. *Travels in North America, in the Years 1827 and 1828.* Edinburgh: Cadell, 1829.

*Hamilton, Thomas. *Men and Manners in America.* London: T. Cadell, 1833.

King, Edward. *The Great South*. 1879, reprint. Edited by W. Magruder Drake and Robert R. Jones. Baton Rouge: Louisiana State University Press, 1972.

Levasseur, A. *LaFayette in America in 1824 and 1825; or, Journal of a Voyage to the United States*. Translated by John D. Godman. Philadelphia: Carey & Lea, 1829.

Lyell, Sir Charles. *A Second Visit to the United States of North America*. New York: Harper & Brothers, 1850.

*Martineau, Harriet. *Society in America*. London: Saunders & Otley, 1837.

Mereness, Newton D., ed. *Travels in the American Colonies*. 1916, reprint. New York: Antiquarian Press, 1961.

Olmsted, Frederick Law. *A Journey in the Seaboard Slave States*. New York: Dix and Edwards, 1856.

Pope, John. *A Tour through the Southern and Western Territories of the United States of North-America*. Richmond: John Dixon, 1792.

*Power, Tyrone. *Impressions of America during the Years 1833, 1834, & 1835*. London: Richard Bentley, 1836.

Russell, William Howard. *My Diary North and South*. Boston: T.O.H.P. Burnham, 1863.

Sims, J. Marion. *The Story of My Life*. Edited by H. Marion Sims. New York: D. Appleton, 1894.

*Stuart, James. *Three Years in North America*. 2d ed., revised. Edinburgh: R. Cadell, 1833.

Tocqueville, Alexis de. *Democracy in America*. Translated by Henry Reeve. Original preface and notes by John C. Spencer. New York: Adlard and Saunders, 1838 [first American edition]. (See, also, Tocqueville, Alexis de. *Journey to America*. Edited by J. P. Mayer. Translated by George Lawrence. Revised and augmented edition in collaboration with A. P. Kerr. Anchor Books. Garden City: Doubleday, 1971.)

Other References

Goff, John H. "Excursion Along an Old Way to the West." *Georgia Review* 6 (Summer 1952): 188-202.

Hamilton, Peter Joseph. "Early Roads of Alabama." *Transactions of the Alabama Historical Society, 1897-1898* 2:39-56.

Martin, William Elejius. "Internal Improvements in Alabama." *Johns Hopkins University Studies in Historical and Political Science*. Series 20, No. 4 (April 1902).

Renfro, N. P., Jr. "The Beginning of Railroads in Alabama." *Alabama Polytechnic Institute Historical Studies*. 4th Series. Auburn, Alabama, 1910.

----

*Introduced and excerpted in Walter Brownlow Posey, ed. *Alabama in the 1830's As Recorded by British Travellers. Birmingham-Southern College Bulletin* 31:4 (December 1938).

Between the Lines*

LEE SMITH

Literary genius can be recognized but hardly defined; it is marked by energy, by the ability to make the familiar become fresh, and by the possession of a vision that gives to characters and settings a new context. Whatever else may be said to define genius, Lee Smith's fiction exhibits all of the above. Her fine ear for speech makes characters who are neighbor and kin to all in the rural South take on new life, and her energy is displayed in each new creation. Her fifth novel, *Oral History*, was published in 1983 to excellent reviews and a slot as a Literary Guild alternate. Her short stories have appeared in national magazines, among them *Redbook* and *McCall's*, and two have received O. Henry Prizes.

*Reprinted by permission of G. P. Putnam's Sons from *Cakewalk* by Lee Smith. Copyright © 1981 by Lee Smith.

One of those award-winning stories, "Between the Lines," is the product of the author's Alabama experience. The idea for writing from the point of view of Mrs. Joline B. Newhouse came to Lee Smith when she was a reporter for *The Tuscaloosa News* in the early 1970s and an occasional editor of "country correspondence." Her three years in Alabama influenced other stories and resulted in a comic masterpiece, the novel *Fancy Strut* (1974). The author gives credit to Southern literary critic Louis D. Rubin, Jr., her mentor at Hollins College, for encouraging her to write about a South she knew. Any Alabama reader familiar with "country correspondence" will know the speaker in "Between the Lines" and may agree that sweet potatoes have not tasted the same since man landed on the moon.

"PEACE BE WITH YOU from Mrs. Joline B. Newhouse" is how I sign my columns. Now I gave some thought to that. In the first place, I like a line that has a ring to it. In the second place, what I have always tried to do with my column is to uplift my readers if at all possible, which sometimes it is not. After careful thought, I threw out "Yours in Christ." I am a religious person and all my readers know it. If I put "Yours in Christ," it seems to me that they will think I am theirs because I am in Christ, or even that they and I are in Christ *together*, which is not always the case. I am in Christ but I know for a fact that a lot of them are not. There's no use acting like they are, but there's no use rubbing their faces in it, either. "Peace be with you," as I see it, is sufficiently religious without laying all the cards right out on the table in plain view. I like to keep an ace or two up my sleeve. I like to write between the lines.

This is what I call my column, in fact: "Between the Lines, by Mrs. Joline B. Newhouse." Nobody knows why. Many people have come right out and asked me, including my best friend, Sally Peck, and my husband, Glenn. "Come on, now, Joline," they say. "What's this 'Between the Lines' all about? What's this 'Between the Lines' supposed to mean?" But I just smile a sweet mysterious smile and change the subject. I know what I know.

And my column means everything to folks around here. Salt Lick community is where we live, unincorporated. I guess there is not much that you would notice, passing through—the Post Office (real little), the American oil station, my husband Glenn's Cash 'N Carry Beverage Store. He sells more than beverages in there, though, believe me. He sells everything you can think of, from thermometers and rubbing alcohol to nails to frozen pizza. Anything else you want, you have to go out of the holler and get on the interstate and go to Greenville to get it. That's where my column appears, in the *Greenville Herald*, fortnightly. Now there's a word with a ring to it: fortnightly.

There are seventeen families here in Salt Lick—twenty, if you count those three down by the Five Mile Bridge. I put what they do in the paper. Anybody gets married, I write it. That goes for born, divorced, dies, celebrates a golden wedding anniversary, has a baby shower, visits relatives in Ohio, you name it. But these mere facts are not what's most important, to my mind.

I write, for instance: "Mrs. Alma Goodnight is enjoying a pleasant recuperation period in the lovely, modern Walker Mountain Community Hospital while she is sorely missed by her loved ones at home. Get well soon, Alma!" I do not write that Alma Goodnight is in the hospital because her husband hit her up the side with a rake and left a straight line of bloody little holes going from her waist to her armpit after she yelled at him, which Lord knows she did all the time, once too often. I don't write about how Eben Goodnight is all torn up now about what he did, missing work and worrying, or how Alma likes it so much in the hospital that nobody knows if they'll ever get her to go home or not. Because that is a *mystery*, and I am no detective by a long shot. I am what I am, I know what I know, and I know you've got to give folks something to hang on to, something to keep them going. That is what I have in mind when I say *uplift*, and that is what God had in mind when he gave us Jesus Christ.

My column would not be but a paragraph if the news was all I told. But it isn't. What I tell is what's important, like the bulbs coming up, the way the redbud comes out first on the hills in the spring and how pretty it looks, the way the cattails shoot up by the creek, how the mist winds down low on the ridge in the mornings, how my wash all hung out on the line on a Tuesday looks like a regular square dance with those pants legs just flapping and flapping in the wind! I tell how all the things you ever dreamed of, all changed and ghostly, will come crowding into your head on a winter night when you sit up late in front of your fire. I even made up these little characters to talk for me, Mr. and Mrs. Cardinal and Princess Pussycat, and often I have them voice my thoughts. Each week I give a little chapter in their lives. Or I might tell what was the message brought in church, or relate an inspirational word from a magazine, book, or TV. I look on the bright side of life.

I've had God's gift of writing from the time I was a child. That's what the B. stands for in Mrs. Joline B. Newhouse—Barker, my maiden name. My father was a patient strong God-fearing man despite his problems and it is in his honor that I maintain the B. There was a lot of us children around all the time—it was right up the road here where I grew up—and it would take me a day to tell you what all we got into! But after I learned how to write, that was that. My fingers just naturally curved to a pencil and I sat down to writing like a ball of fire. They skipped me up one, two grades in school. When I was not but eight, I wrote a poem named "God's Garden," which was published in the church bulletin of the little Methodist Church we went to then on Hunter's Ridge. Oh, Daddy was so proud! He gave me a quarter that Sunday, and then I turned around and gave it straight to God. Put it in the collection plate. Daddy almost cried he was so proud. I wrote another poem in school the next year, telling how life is like a maple tree, and it won a statewide prize.

That's me—I grew up smart as a whip, lively, and naturally good. Jesus came as easy as breathing did to me. Don't think I'm putting on airs, though: I'm not. I know what I know. I've done my share of sinning, too, of which more later.

Anyway, I was smart. It's no telling but what I might have gone on to school like my own children have and who knows what all else if Mama hadn't run off with a man. I don't remember Mama very well, to tell the truth. She was a weak woman, always laying in the bed having a headache. One day we all came home from school and she was gone, didn't even bother to make up the bed. Well, that was the end of Mama! None of us ever saw her again, but

Daddy told us right before he died that one time he had gotten a postcard from her from Atlanta, Georgia, years and years after that. He showed it to us, all wrinkled and soft from him holding it.

Being the oldest, I took over and raised those little ones, three of them, and then I taught school and then I married Glenn and we had our own children, four of them, and I have raised them too and still have Marshall, of course, poor thing. He is the cross I have to bear and he'll be just like he is now for the rest of his natural life.

I was writing my column for the week of March 17, 1976, when the following events occurred. It was a real coincidence because I had just finished doing the cutest little story named "A Red-Letter Day for Mr. and Mrs. Cardinal" when the phone rang. It rings all the time, of course. Everybody around here knows my number by heart. It was Mrs. Irene Chalmers. She was all torn up. She said that Mr. Biggers was over at Greenville at the hospital very bad off this time, and that he was asking for me and would I please try to get over there today as the doctors were not giving him but a twenty percent chance to make it through the night. Mr. Biggers has always been a fan of mine, and he especially liked Mr. and Mrs. Cardinal. "Well!" I said. "Of course I will! I'll get Glenn on the phone right this minute. And you calm down, Mrs. Chalmers. You go fix yourself a Coke." Mrs. Chalmers said she would and hung up. I knew what was bothering her, of course. It was that given the natural run of things, she would be the next to go. The next one to be over there dying. Without even putting down the receiver, I dialed the beverage store. Bert answered.

"Good morning," I said. I like to maintain a certain distance with the hired help although Glenn does not. He will talk to anybody, and any time you go in there, you can find half the old men in the county just sitting around that stove in the winter or outside on those wooden drink boxes in the summer, smoking and drinking drinks which I am sure they are getting free out of the cooler although Glenn swears it on the Bible they are not. Anyway, I said good morning.

"Can I speak to Glenn?" I said.

"Well, now, Mrs. Newhouse," Bert said in his naturally insolent voice—he is just out of high school and too big for his britches—"he's not here right now. He had to go out for a while."

"Where did he go?" I asked.

"Well, I don't rightly know," Bert said. "He said he'd be back after lunch."

"Thank you very much, there will not be a message," I said sweetly, and hung up. I *knew* where Glenn was. Glenn was over on Caney Creek where his adopted half-sister Margie Kettles lived, having carnal knowledge of her in the trailer. They had been at it for thirty years and anybody would have thought they'd have worn it out by that time. Oh, I knew all about it.

The way it happened in the beginning was that Glenn's father had died of his lungs when Glenn was not but about ten years old, and his mother grieved so hard that she went off her head and began taking up with anybody who would go with her. One of the fellows she took up with was a foreign man out of a carnival, the James H. Drew Exposition, a man named Emilio something. He had this curly-headed dark-skinned little daughter. So Emilio stayed around longer than anybody would have expected, but finally it was clear to all that he never would find any work around here to suit him. The work around here is hard work, all of it, and they say he played a musical instrument. Anyway, in due course this Emilio just up and vanished, leaving that foreign child. Now that was Margie, of course, but her name wasn't Margie then. It was a long foreign name, which ended up as Margie, and that's how Margie ended up here, in these mountains, where she has been up to no good ever since. Glenn's mother did not last too long after Emilio left, and those children grew up wild. Most of them went to foster homes, and to this day Glenn does not know where two of his brothers are! The military was what finally saved Glenn. He stayed with the military for nine years, and when he came back to this area he found me over here teaching school and with something of a nest egg in hand, enabling him to start the beverage store. Glenn says he owes everything to me.

This is true. But I can tell you something else: Glenn is a good man, and he has been a good provider all these years. He has never spoken to me above a regular tone of voice nor raised his hand in anger. He has not been tight with the money. He used to hold the girls in his lap of an evening. Since I got him started, he has been a regular member of the church, and he has not fallen down on it yet. Glenn furthermore has that kind of disposition where he never knows a stranger. So I can count my blessings, too.

Of course I knew about Margie! Glenn's sister Lou-Ann told me about it before she died, that is how I found out about it originally. She thought I *should* know, she said. She said it went on for years and she just wanted me to know before she died. Well! I had had the first two girls by then, and I thought I was so happy. I took to my bed and just cried and cried. I cried for four days and then by gum I got up and started my column, and I have been writing on it ever since. So I was not unprepared when Margie showed up again some years after that, all gap-toothed and wild-looking but then before you knew it she was gone, off again to Knoxville, then back working as a waitress at that truck stop at the county line, then off again, like that. She led an irregular life. And as for Glenn, I will have to hand it to him, he never darkened her door again until after the birth of Marshall.

Now let me add that I would not have gone on and had Marshall if it was left up to me. I would have practiced more birth control. Because I was old by that time, thirty-seven, and that was too old for more children I felt, even though I had started late of course. I had told Glenn many times, I said three normal girls is enough for anybody. But no, Glenn was like a lot of men, and I don't blame him for it—he just had to try one more time for a boy. So we went on with it, and I must say I had a feeling all along.

I was not a bit surprised at what we got, although after wrestling with it all for many hours in the dark night of the soul, as they say, I do not believe that Marshall is a judgment on me for my sin. I don't believe that. He is one of God's special children, is how I look at it. Of course he looks funny, but he has already lived ten years longer than they said he would. And has a job! He goes to Greenville every day on the Trailways bus, rain or shine, and cleans up the Plaza Mall. He gets to ride on the bus, and he gets to see people. Along about six o'clock he'll come back, walking up the holler and not looking to one side or the other, and then I give him his supper and then he'll watch something on TV like "The Brady Bunch" or "Family Affair," and then he'll go to bed. He would not hurt a flea. But oh, Glenn took it hard when Marshall came! I remember that night so well and the way he just turned his back on the doctor. This is what sent him back to Margie, I am convinced of it, what made him take up right where he had left off all those years before.

So since Glenn was up to his old tricks I called up Lavonne, my daughter, to see if she could take me to the hospital to see Mr. Biggers. Why yes she could, it turned out. As a matter of fact she was going to Greenville herself. As a matter of fact she had something she wanted to talk to me about anyway. Now Lavonne is our youngest girl and the only one that stayed around here. Lavonne is somewhat pop-eyed and has a weak constitution. She is one of those people that never can make up their minds. That day on the phone, I heard a whine in her voice I didn't like the sound of. Something is up, I thought.

First I powdered my face, so I would be ready to go when Lavonne got here. Then I sat back down to write some more on my column, this paragraph I had been framing in my mind for weeks about how sweet potatoes are not what they used to be. They taste gritty and dry now, compared to how they were. I don't know the cause of it, whether it is man on the moon or pollution in the ecology or what, but it is true. They taste awful.

Then my door came bursting open in a way that Lavonne would never do it and I knew it was Sally Peck from next door. Sally is loud and excitable but she has a good heart. She would do anything for you. "Hold on to your hat, Joline!" she hollered. Sally is so loud because she's deaf. Sally was just huffing and puffing—she is a heavy woman—and she had rollers still up in her hair and her old housecoat on with the buttons off.

"Why, Sally!" I exclaimed. "You are all wrought up!"

Sally sat down in my rocker and spread out her legs and started fanning herself with my *Family Circle* magazine. "If you think I'm wrought up," she said finally, "it is nothing compared to what you are going to be. We have had us a suicide, right here in Salt Lick. Margie Kettles put her head inside her gas oven in the night."

"Margie?" I said. My heart was just pumping.

"Yes, and a little neighbor girl was the one who found her, they say. She went over to borrow some baking soda for her mama's biscuits at seven o'clock A.M." Sally looked real hard at me. "Now wasn't she related to you all?"

"Why," I said just as easily, "why yes, she was Glenn's adopted half-sister of course when they were nothing but a child. But we haven't had anything to do with her for years as you can well imagine."

"Well, they say Glenn is making the burial arrangements," Sally spoke up. She was getting her own back that day, I'll admit it. Usually I'm the one with all the news.

"I have to finish my column now and then Lavonne is taking me in to Greenville to see old Mr. Biggers who is breathing his last," I said.

"Well," Sally said, hauling herself up out of my chair, "I'll be going along then. I just didn't know if you knew it or not." Now Sally Peck is not a spiteful woman in all truth. I have known her since we were little girls sitting out in the yard looking at a magazine together. It is hard to imagine being as old as I am now, or knowing Sally Peck—who was Sally Bland then—so long.

Of course I couldn't get my mind back on sweet potatoes after she left. I just sat still and fiddled with the pigeonholes in my desk and the whole kitchen seemed like it was moving and rocking back and forth around me. Margie dead! Sooner or later I would have to tastefully write it up in my column. Well, I must say I had never thought of Margie dying. Before God, I never hoped for that in all my life. I didn't know what it would do to *me*, in fact, to me and Glenn and Marshall and the way we live because you know how the habits and the ways of people can build up over the years. It was too much for me to take in at one time. I couldn't see how anybody committing suicide could choose to stick their head in the oven anyway—you can imagine the position you would be found in.

Well, in came Lavonne at that point, sort of hanging back and stuttering like she always does, and that child of hers Bethy Rose hanging on to her skirt for dear life. I saw no reason at that time to tell Lavonne about the death of Margie Kettles. She would hear it sooner or later, anyway. Instead, I gave her some plant food that I had ordered two for the price of one from Montgomery Ward some days before.

"Are you all ready, Mama?" Lavonne asked in that quavery way she has, and I said indeed I was, as soon as I got my hat, which I did, and we went out and got in Lavonne's Buick Electra and set off on our trip. Bethy Rose sat in the back, coloring in her coloring book. She is a real good child. "How's Ron?" I said. Ron is Lavonne's husband, an electrician, as up and coming a boy as you would want to see. Glenn and I are as proud as punch of Ron, and actually I never have gotten over the shock of Lavonne marrying him in the first place. All through high school she never showed any signs of marrying anybody, and you could have knocked me over with a feather the day she told us she was secretly engaged. I'll tell you, our Lavonne was not the marrying sort! Or so I thought.

But that day in the car she told me, "Mama, I wanted to talk to you and tell you I am thinking of getting a d-i-v-o-r-c-e."

I shot a quick look into the back seat but Bethy Rose wasn't hearing a thing. She was coloring Wonder Woman in her book.

"Now, Lavonne," I said. "What in the world is it? Why, I'll bet you can work it out." Part of me was listening to Lavonne, as you can imagine, but part of me was still stuck in that oven with crazy Margie. I was not myself.

I told her that. "Lavonne," I said, "I am not myself today. But I'll tell you one thing. You give this some careful thought. You don't want to go off half-cocked. What is the problem, anyway?"

"It's a man where I work," Lavonne said. She works in the Welfare Department, part-time, typing. "He is just giving me a fit. I guess you can pray for me, Mama, because I don't know what I'll decide to do."

"Can we get an Icee?" asked Bethy Rose.

"Has anything happened between you?" I asked. You have to get all the facts.

"Why, no!" Lavonne was shocked. "Why, I wouldn't do anything like that! Mama, for goodness' sakes! We just have coffee together so far."

That's Lavonne all over. She never has been very bright. "Honey," I said, "I would think twice before I threw up a perfectly good marriage and a new brick home for the sake of a cup of coffee. If you don't have enough to keep you busy, go take a course at the community college. Make yourself a new pantsuit. This is just a mood, believe me."

"Well," Lavonne said. Her voice was shaking and her eyes were swimming in tears that just stayed there and never rolled down her cheeks. "Well," she said again.

As for me, I was lost in thought. It was when I was a young married woman like Lavonne that I committed my own great sin. I had the girls, and things were fine with Glenn and all, and there was simply not any reason to ascribe to it. It was just something I did out of loving pure and simple, did because I wanted to do it. I knew and have always known the consequences, yet God is full of grace, I pray and believe, and his mercy is everlasting.

To make a long story short, we had a visiting evangelist from Louisville, Kentucky, for a two-week revival that year. John Marcel Wilkes. If I say it myself, John Marcel Wilkes was a real humdinger! He had the yellowest hair you ever saw, curly, and the finest singing voice available. Oh, he was something, and that very first night he brought two souls into Christ. The next day I went over to the church with a pan of brownies just to tell him how much I personally had received from his message. I thought, of course, that there would be other people around—the Reverend Mr. Clark, or the youth director, or somebody cleaning. But to my surprise that church was totally empty except for John Marcel Wilkes himself reading the Bible in the fellowship hall and making notes on a pad of paper. The sun came in a window on his head. It was early June, I remember, and I had on a blue dress with little white cap sleeves and open-toed sandals. John Marcel Wilkes looked up at me and his face gave off light like the sun.

"Why, Mrs. Newhouse," he said. "What an unexpected pleasure!" His voice echoed out in the empty fellowship hall. He had the most beautiful voice, too—strong and deep, like it had bells in it. Everything he said had a ring to it.

He stood up and came around the table to where I was. I put the brownies down on the table and stood there. We both just stood there, real close without touching each other, for the longest time, looking into each other's eyes. Then he took my hands and brought them up to his mouth and kissed them, which nobody ever did to me before or since, and then he kissed me on the mouth. I thought I would die. After some time of that, we went together out into the hot June day where the bees were all buzzing around the flowers there by the back gate and I couldn't think straight. "Come," said John Marcel Wilkes. We went out in the woods behind the church to the prettiest place, and when it was all over I could look up across his curly yellow head and over the trees and see the white church steeple stuck up against that blue, blue sky like it was pasted there. This was not all. Two more times we went out there during that revival. John Marcel Wilkes left after that and I have never heard a word of him in all these years. I do know that I never bake a pan of brownies, or hear the church bells ring, but what I think of him. So I have to pity Lavonne and her cup of coffee if you see what I mean, just like I have to spend the rest of my life to live my sinning down. But I'll tell you this: if I had it all to do over, I would do it all over again, and I would not trade it in for anything.

Lavonne drove off to look at fabric and get Bethy Rose an Icee, and I went in the hospital. I hate the way they smell. As soon as I entered Mr. Biggers' room, I could see he was breathing his last. He was so tiny in the bed you almost missed him, a poor little shriveled-up thing. His family sat all around.

"Aren't you sweet to come?" they said. "Looky here, honey, it's Mrs. Newhouse."

He didn't move a muscle, all hooked up to tubes. You could hear him breathing all over the room.

"It's Mrs. Newhouse," they said, louder. "Mrs. Newhouse is here. Last night he was asking for everybody," they said to me. "Now he won't open his eyes. You are real sweet to come," they said. "You certainly did brighten his days." Now I knew this was true because the family had remarked on it before.

"I'm so glad," I said. Then some more people came in the door and everybody was talking at once, and while they were doing that, I went over to the bed and got right up by his ear.

"Mr. Biggers!" I said. "Mr. Biggers, it's Joline Newhouse here."

He opened one little old bleary eye.

"Mr. Biggers!" I said right into his ear. "Mr. Biggers, you know those cardinals in my column? Mr. and Mrs. Cardinal? Well, I made them up! I made them up, Mr. Biggers. They never were real at all." Mr. Biggers closed his eyes and a nurse came in and I stood up.

"Thank you so much for coming, Mrs. Newhouse," his daughter said.

"He is one fine old gentleman," I told them all, and then I left.

Outside in the hall, I had to lean against the tile wall for support while I waited for the elevator to come. Imagine, me saying such a thing to a dying man! I was not myself that day.

Lavonne took me to the big Kroger's in north Greenville and we did our shopping, and on the way back in the car she told me she had been giving everything a lot of thought and she guessed I was right after all.

"You're not going to tell anybody, are you?" she asked me anxiously, popping her eyes. "You're not going to tell Daddy, are you?" she said.

"Why, Lord no, honey!" I told her. "It is the farthest thing from my mind."

Sitting in the back seat among all the grocery bags, Bethy Rose sang a little song she had learned at school. "Make new friends but keep the old, some are silver but the other gold," she sang.

"I don't know what I was thinking of," Lavonne said.

Glenn was not home yet when I got there—making his arrangements, I supposed. I took off my hat, made myself a cup of Sanka, and sat down and finished off my column on a high inspirational note, saving Margie and Mr. Biggers for the next week. I cooked up some ham and red-eye gravy, which Glenn just loves, and then I made some biscuits. The time seemed to pass so slow. The phone rang two times while I was fixing supper, but I just let it go. I thought I had received enough news for *that* day. I still couldn't get over Margie putting her head in the oven, or what I said to poor Mr. Biggers, which was not at all like me you can be sure. I buzzed around that kitchen doing first one thing, then another. I couldn't keep my mind on anything I did.

After a while Marshall came home, and ate, and went in the front room to watch TV. He cannot keep it in his head that watching TV in the dark will ruin your eyes, so I always have to go in there and turn on a light for him. This night, though, I didn't. I just let him sit there in the recliner in the dark, watching his show, and in the pale blue light from that TV set he looked just like anybody else.

I put on a sweater and went out on the front porch and sat in the swing to watch for Glenn. It was nice weather for that time of year, still a little cold but you could smell spring in the air already and I knew it wouldn't be long before the redbud would come out again on the hills. Out in the dark where I couldn't see them, around the front steps, my crocuses were already up. After a while of sitting out there I began to take on a chill, due more to my age no doubt than the weather, but just then some lights came around the bend, two headlights, and I knew it was Glenn coming home.

Glenn parked the truck and came up the steps. He was dog-tired, I could see that. He came over to the swing and put his hand on my shoulder. A little wind came up, and by then it was so dark you could see lights on all the ridges where the people live. "Well, Joline," he said.

"Dinner is waiting on you," I said. "You go in and wash up and I'll be there directly. I was getting worried about you," I said.

Glenn went on and I sat there swaying on the breeze for a minute before I went after him. Now where will it all end? I ask you. All this pain and loving, mystery and loss. And it just goes on and on, from Glenn's mother taking up with dark-skinned gypsies to my own daddy and his postcard to that silly Lavonne and her cup of coffee to Margie with her head in the oven, to John Marcel Wilkes and myself, God help me, and all of it so long ago out in those holy woods.

Lella Warren's

Literary Gift—

Alabama

NANCY G. ANDERSON

A native Mississippian, Nancy G. Anderson graduated *magna cum laude* from Millsaps College with a degree in English. She attended the University of Virginia on a DuPont Fellowship and received an M.A. in English. After graduate school, she was named head of the English department at Frankfurt (Germany) International School. She is currently director of composition at Auburn University at Montgomery, where she has been a member of the English department since 1973. Her teaching responsibilities are primarily in the writing program with an occasional special course in the historical novel that allows her to combine two fields of interest—history and the novel. Professor Anderson first heard Lella Warren's name, not in Alabama, in Mississippi, or even in the South, but in Princeton, New Jersey. A retired editor with Princeton University Press, learning Anderson was from Alabama, asked whether she had read the novels of Lella Warren.

The look of disbelief at her negative response prompted Anderson to return to Alabama and correct the oversight. When Lella Warren died in 1982, her daughter, Lee Spanogle Shipman, and husband, Buel W. Patch, delivered the manuscript collection to Anderson for inventory and cataloguing. A primary goal of Nancy Anderson's work in this area is to get unpublished works by Warren into print and to encourage republication of the novels—especially those about Alabama.

LELLA WARREN was born in Clayton, Alabama, in 1899, but she did not initially write about the state that eventually became a setting, even a force, in her writings. When she did finally turn to her birthplace—and the family lore associated with it—the result was the best-selling *Foundation Stone*.

The success of this novel that told of the settling of Alabama was immediate and extensive. The novel was in its third printing prior to its release date of 9 September 1940 and had sold over 30,000 copies by 13 October 1940. There were eventually fourteen printings, a Canadian edition, a British edition, a Grosset & Dunlap reprint, a condensed version in *Omnibook* in January 1941, and translations into Danish and Portuguese. It was on the best-seller lists through the fall, winter, and spring of 1940 and 1941, reaching tenth place by 5 October 1940, and it eventually climbed as high as second place on lists with Thomas Wolfe's *You Can't Go Home Again*, Ernest Hemingway's *For Whom the Bell Tolls*, Thomas Mann's *The Beloved Returns*, Richard Llewellyn's *How Green Was My Valley*, and Jan Struther's *Mrs. Miniver*. *Whetstone Walls* (1952), the sequel to *Foundation Stone*, did not have the extensive success of the earlier novel, but was also in its third printing prior to release. Undoubtedly, Lella Warren's works that use the history of her home state, the spirit of its people, and the legends of her family as setting and subject were her most successful. However, she had written for many years before she achieved such popularity.

Lella Warren began writing when she was about eight years old, but Alabama did not figure in these early works. She once stated her reason for writing: "I write . . . because I discovered as a child that I could create a three-dimensional world on two-dimensional paper, with alive people moving around. As I grew beyond those childhood writing years, spent in an old Morris chair with a stack of paper and a stack of ginger snaps and a free Saturday, I discovered further that I wanted to make this aliveness of my people lasting. To impart it to others." This premise imbued her early works with more emphasis on character than setting.

When Lella Warren's first novel, *A Touch of Earth*, was published by Simon & Schuster in 1926, it was successful enough for a Grosset & Dunlap reprint in 1931 and successful enough to enable Warren to make money by publishing articles and short stories in the popular magazines of the 1920s and 1930s—*Cosmopolitan, Good Housekeeping, Collier's, College Humor, Story*. The Alfred A. Knopf publicity release for *Foundation Stone* described the Lella Warren of this earlier period as "a prosperous young writer for the boom-time 'slicks,' and [she was] getting a little tired of turning out smooth and meaningless stories written to formula." In 1940, Warren concluded that: "A few of the things I wrote had some merit and showed some advance, but most of it soon became tripe." As late as 1976 in an autobiographical essay, she described some of these works as "rather trivial."

But the novel, essays, and stories of this period deserve attention. *A Touch of Earth*, "autobiographical in tone and feeling, though not in events," tells of the struggles and frustrations of Jill Ingel Cheney Kent ("Jick") as she grows up, marries, and aspires to become a writer. As reviews noted, the style of writing in the novel becomes more sophisticated as "Jick" matures and develops her writing skills. The stories of the 1920s and 1930s revolve around such subjects as love or a love triangle, childhood and adolescence, and family relationships. There is often an indefinite Southern setting or a suggestion of a Southern atmosphere, but no identifiable or specific sense of place. Lella Warren wrote nonfiction articles about her alma mater (George Washington University), life in various cities in which she had lived, and the preflight preparations of Charles Lindbergh, an article personally edited by the aviator.

Not satisfied with her writing at this time, despite its merit, Lella Warren (according to the Knopf release) "wanted something big enough to really sink her teeth into, difficult enough to challenge her talents, important enough in its meaning for America to demand of her the best that was in her." Warren's father, Dr. Benjamin Smart Warren, had always encouraged his daughter to set high goals for her writing and to strive to achieve them. In "Born Patriarch," an unpublished work about her father, the daughter records his comments on this subject: "Well it was worth saving your life for, Lella [she was critically ill in the early 1930s], if you're going to write good and plain. . . . But I feel kinder sorry for you . . . you're such an idealist. I only hope you don't have to pay *too* hard and too *long* for your ideals. . . . That's all right, *if* you can look your ideals square in the face, and know what they're bound to cost you. . . . don't let any of the family, or others, get your goat about your writing. *Stick to it along the lines that we've discussed, that you know are right for you.* Even if the money doesn't come in easily."

In those discussions, Dr. Warren often urged his daughter to write of the "true South" that they both knew, not the stereotypical South of mint juleps and magnolias. Although Dr. Warren's work with the U.S. Public Health Service had taken him and his family away from Alabama when Lella was only a small child, he instilled a sense of place and of loyalty to family and family origins. In 1952, Lella Warren wrote: "Our continent-trotting life was off-set by leisurely visits back down home, to make sure that our transplanted roots could still burrow back into native red clay and flourish." Thus, Warren turned to the state of her birth and the stories and traditions of the pioneering ancestors of her family for her setting and her subject. She devoted twelve years to researching historical texts, nineteenth-century Alabama newspapers, and family diaries, letters, wills, and the oral tradition for the setting of the first of these Alabama historical novels, *Foundation Stone*, and a similar period to its sequel, *Whetstone Walls*. As the Knopf publicity indicated, she wanted "To get all the facts—not only the incidents that lived in family legend, but that vast quantity on the lay of the land a century ago, the ways of the settlers and their Indian neighbors, and all the rest of the thousand and one details which make up a vanished way of living." Lella Warren blended these details of Alabama's history with the stories of her ancestors for the nucleus of *Foundation Stone* and *Whetstone Walls*. After years of apprenticeship,

Lella Warren had found the setting and the story that led to her first major success.

In *Foundation Stone,* Yarbrough Whetstone, crossing the Chattahoochee River into Alabama, introduces Alabama into the fiction of Lella Warren as he first views this wilderness:

> "Over there that's *Alabama!*"
> Everyone in his little company scamped on breakfast, being eager to set foot on Alabama soil. They were somewhat delayed, however, for quite a collection of riders, wagons, and other vehicles were waiting in the churned-up mud by the river bank. So the sun was well up before their turn came for the Indian to ferry them across. All fell silent as they passed mid-stream. They had come a long way to reach this land. . . .
> For an hour they rode on, making about four miles through a forest of pines that now showed many lofty hickories and oaks as well. They came into a clearing and Yarbrough had his first vast view of the plateau. A vista stretched away into majesty. He felt dwarfed, yet also strangely like some lonely patriarch of old. . . .
> Yarbrough went a little way apart and leaned against a tall tree-trunk, his arms folded to rest the sag of his weary shoulders. Through a gap he could glimpse a lift of sky. The trees seemed to roar up against it. Up! Everything seemed on high here. Not a single peak, but the whole land was held above the place where the earth had been before. It would take large men to set foot upon it and stay. . . .
> The half-light fell through the trees. An owl hooted. Unknown creatures scuffed in the underbrush. It was the wilderness!

After selecting the site for the new Whetstone home, Yarbrough leaves some members of his scouting expedition in Alabama to clear land and begin breaking ground while he returns to his once-prosperous South Carolina plantation for his youthful wife, Gerda van Ifort Whetstone, and his family. Gerda, based on Warren's "forceful great-grandmother," Lucinda Ifort Warren, is the foundation stone of this Alabama pioneering clan. Just as Yarbrough's apprehensions had vanished when he stood in this Alabama wilderness, so Gerda's initial fears fade, as if she too draws strength from the land:

She made her way through the stumps toward a higher hummock of ground, overgrown with some sort of vine. It gave on a little gap between tall pine trees, where she stood filling her lungs. The leaves of the vine were coated with dew, making it shimmer like frost, and some berries were picked out bright against it here and there. The trees around were big-girthed, and shot high into the air. In the gap the sky showed white with the day that was waiting behind it. And the morning star hung very big and clear, about to set.

Gerda thought: "There's something free and new here, and this will be more *my* land because I helped to start it." The Home Place had already been shaped by other hands. It was only a trust, loaned to her for a short space. This would be hers, as much of it as she could put her mark upon.

Lella Warren must have imbued her fictional creation of Gerda with some of her own personal feelings as she wrote about her state, to "put her mark upon" [it] and to capture this state and its people for her readers.

The affairs of the Whetstone clan are part of the development of Alabama. Lella Warren wanted to recreate the pioneering days of this state because she believed this period had never received detailed, accurate, effective treatment in fiction. The results of her research—never abstract—allow readers to see concrete circumstances defining pioneer life:

Summer came with a lush heat such as Gerda had never felt even in her first Southern summer at the Home Place. Here it was tropical. Their small clearing was shut in by a dense wall of forest that required chopping with an ax to penetrate any great distance. Pines, hickories, sweet gum, and water oaks rose to heights well over a hundred feet, with Spanish-moss ropes lacing together the top branches and underbrush, choking out all air below, making their shade stifling rather than cool. Gnats and mosquitoes swarmed so thickly that the children, coming back from exploring the edge of the woods, were bitten and swollen like grotesque puffballs, and Pokey had to rub them with camphor grease to keep them from scratching themselves raw. All grew heartily weary of the long-drawn-out endlessness of summer.

The corn in such fields as had been cleared, however, throve in the simmer of sun and the fall of rain, shooting up to enormous green heights, heavy with well-filled ears. Corn was their main crop these first pioneering years. It was eaten green as a vegetable, dried for winter use, pounded into hominy, ground into meal, used for bartering, depended upon heavily, and despised passionately by Gracey and Miz Lisbeth [Yarbrough's sister and mother].

Oddly enough, the cotton for which they had made this migration from an old and well-established ease into a hazardous discomfort was relegated to a minor place for the time being. There were as yet no other places where its value could have been realized. Therefore at first each family raised only enough for its domestic use on the plantation. Having no cotton gins here, the lint had to be picked off tediously by hand from the seed, the children helping. The seed was dumped into ditches to put it out of the way.

Gradually the Whetstones, their relatives, and their neighbors prosper in this new land, but the prosperity yields moral complications. They work with, and on occasion against, the Creek Indians. Yarbrough goes to Tuscaloosa to hear the farewell speech of Chief Yufala to the Alabama legislature, delivered "with what irony we cannot know, not being of the face that was stilled into a bronze immobility the better to bear annihilation." After the speech, a troubled Yarbrough returns home, "thinking of the great hazards that man must encounter in removing a whole tribe into a totally unsettled realm. He was at once grateful for his own more limited responsibility and shamed at the part he and his kind were playing in the eviction called the Treaty of Cession." But Yarbrough's shame is transitory; his seduction of Chief Kocki Fixio's wife betrays his own beliefs, his neighbors, and, of course, Gerda, and it provokes retaliatory conflicts between the Indians and the settlers. Gerda's grandfather and the betrothed of Yarbrough's sister, Gracey, are both killed in these battles. But the Whetstone family survives.

The pattern of prosperity and adversity, rise anticipating fall, is renewed in the flush times of the 1850s:

The decade of the fifties opened with a shout in Alabama. The harsh days of pioneering and Indian-fighting were over, now came a time when its broad half-cleared lands were under the golden reign of King Cotton. The river boats creaked with it, the market-places resounded to the cries of its prices. A black race labored and white lords prospered. The earth burst forth with it, and the sky was filled with clouds upon clouds of white, obscuring all else. It was a time of *Jubilate*!

In Montgomery the new State Capitol stood on Goat Hill above the sprawling town, unkempt, but bursting with its new political importance. Tuscaloosa, the former capital, remained serene behind its high-pillared porches, like some widow that had once known the favor of a robust mate. Mobile was a rowdy waterfront town, with its open square used as a horse and hog pasture, although to the men who came down with their bales for sale it was a colorful place for a fine holiday.

Then came secession and the Civil War with new hardships and a return to some of the struggles of pioneer days. The Whetstones, now including second and third generation Alabamians, suffer losses, but at the end of *Foundation Stone* and throughout *Whetstone Walls*, they continue to work. Ultimately they prosper again as these descendants become physicians, lawyers, businessmen, and farmers, all making their contributions to the state.

Within the panorama of Alabama's history, Lella Warren's characters grow and are sustained from a blend of fact and fiction in the authentic Alabama settings of Eufaula and her birthplace of Clayton, named Turberville in the novels. The growth of the two towns influences, and is influenced by, her characters as they build their towns just as they earlier built their homes. Through the two novels, the settings gradually become charged with age and meaning. Specific details from the original Warren homesite in Clayton, especially the Warren family burying ground and the Rock Wall around the first Warren home, figure strongly. The account of Gerda's retreat to the burying ground for solace was often praised in reviews:

> The next day near its close, she [Gerda] went where she had not gone for a long time, up to the family burying-ground. She turned her eyes in a circle. This was a fine place where she could see far and wide. There was nothing meek about their dead. They were all dressed up in their Sunday best, with rings on their fingers and stick-pins in their shirt bosoms. There were no willows for them either, but the prickle and scarlet of holly, until she felt more like wishing "Christmas gift!" to company than saying prayers for the

dead. And here in their midst she felt like Sister God indeed, standing on a piece of high ground!

In "Born Patriarch," Lella Warren describes her father's reaction when she read to him an early draft of this passage: "Papa's eyes actually got full of tears, which was queer in such a man. Though of course it wasn't altogether my writing that made him cry, it was the fact that I'd made him homesick." There is a note in Warren's handwriting attached to this section: "You must remember that this was written exactly as it happened and almost exactly 15 years ago."

A January 1941 inscription by Lella Warren in a copy of *Foundation Stone* establishes the significance that she attached to the Rock Wall originally built by Lucinda Warren's husband at the Warren homesite, just as Yarbrough builds it around his home: "And more than that the profession of faith that Bruff [Gerda and Yarbrough's oldest son] and Gerda express on 566 *is* Alabama." The story of the wall and of its symbolic meaning is the passage she personally marked on page 566 of that copy:

> . . . instead he [Bruff] swept a hand toward the rock wall.
>
> The eyes of each studied it. The stones had grown coppery with age and deposit, yet there was scarcely a crumbly one among them. Solid, it bent slightly to the natural curve of the land, holding back a lot of wasting down-wash. Then as they looked over its firm brim, they saw how it bulwarked their land, until not even the sky could swallow Whetstone Stand!
>
> Bruff said: "As long as that wall holds, the family will last."
>
> "We will outlast any wall!" Gerda told him, "anywhere. We will build new ones if the old ones have to fall. Our family holds that wall firm, more than it guards the family. No year can come and go with its four seasons that will put an end to our race. I say this who thought I knew death, with Yarbrough."
>
> He put a hand, in faith, on Gerda's shoulder. "I give you my word, Ma'am, the family will go on. Somehow. Through some of us."

This "profession of faith" in the spirit of Alabama is repeated in *Whetstone Walls* as Danley Bruton, Bruff's brother-in-law, ascertains that his nephew, young Rob Whetstone, knows the tradition for which he will be responsible:

> Bro' Danley passed his puckery palms over the flat tawny stones of the wall, and finally asked, "Do you realize that this place where we're sitting, signifies something? I mean this very wall. So thick that it takes four wide stone steps to lead up through it."
>
> Rob clinched the pebbles. "Yes sir, I do. Ma'am Gerda explained it to me. One day during her last spring, when she was putting some powerful big ideas into my head."
>
> "Oh? Then I needn't worry about your not getting ahead. For if Ma'am Gerda singled you out, you'll have to amount to something! And keep this solid." Once more he smoothed the firm step upon which they sat; then went on unable to resist restating what Ma'am had said, now that he had started. "So you know the Wall's story? Of how your Grandfather built it, to prevent this home place from being washed away by any sudden gush or storm? But do you understand the meaning of the story? How none of us it was meant to protect, could by even our own folly destroy what this Wall held secure!" He slammed a fist down hard upon it. "It still holds strong. Yet now—now it's up to you boys to raise the meaning even higher! You must try in any case. Taking account of the shape of the world, upon which this had its spot."

Another portion of the January 1941 inscription refers to the "vigor of Alabama" as described on page 458 of *Foundation Stone*; the passage Warren marked on that page is:

> And what of the men who dwelt in this land, called her their mistress, and gave to this time its flavor, its tone, its shape, its reality?
>
> They were not minted from any single well-worn stamp of high degree. Lordly and humble, they shifted and intermingled, until, without waiting for the passage of a single generation, they became a freshened breed, more vigorous than any of the stocks that went into the making. Virginians, New Englanders, Carolinians, Dutch, Scotch, and even the mercurial Irish strain, mingling in a common conquest, made a high-spirited, stubborn, ruthless race, building prosperity on the foundations of a wilderness. Worrying about malaria and ground itch and schools, knitting their brows over the state of their slaves, visionary about the textile uses of their one staple product, cotton. Dashing, generous, crass perhaps, question-

ing, bombastic. But whatever else they were, they were not of a worn-out vintage of blue blood, past the best year for its consumption by life.

In the inscription, Lella Warren states: "I still hold the essence of this statement to be true."

By the middle of *Whetstone Walls*, Lella Warren's settings begin to move beyond Alabama's boundaries. But whether the characters move to Washington or New Orleans, bonds continue to connect them with their birthplace. Some of the third generation Whetstones leave Alabama, with Rob's going to Tulane Medical School and his brother, Upshur, to the nation's capital to go into business. Upshur sends Rob money for a train ticket so they can have a September reunion in Turberville. After a hasty departure from New Orleans and a long train ride, Rob arrives in Turberville for the unanticipated visit. Like his grandfather and grandmother nearly a century earlier, Rob derives strength from Alabama soil: "He reached down into the soil by the persimmon, and dug up two handfuls of it. Then bent and buried his jawbones against it. 'Good old red clay,' he muttered devoutly."

Even though she left the state as a child, Lella Warren retained her ties with her birthplace, visited when she could, and corresponded with friends and relatives in Clayton. While she was working on *Whetstone Walls*, she wrote a relative in Clayton requesting that she drive out to the Warren homeplace and send details about the fall foliage and fields; Warren obviously was checking the descriptions she was using for Rob's return. An account of her 1952 autograph tour for *Whetstone Walls* mentions an emotional visit to "Ma'am Gerda's grave." In the room where she wrote until her death hung a framed literary map of Alabama. No matter how far Lella Warren—or her characters—moved away, or how long they were gone, the spirit and strength of Alabama went with them and remained a touchstone in their lives. A summary of the planned sequel for *Whetstone Walls* captures the relationship of the state to the distant settings:

> THIS, OUR COUNTRY—The telling of the tale of the next two generations of this family, who trampled so hard upon the heels of their parents, that they all but crumbled some of the walls of these

ramparts. Yet who in the end dared again, labored long, and died often—that not only *their* House should stand fast, but that *this, our country* could become the lodestone upon which *all mankind could found shelter for its varying dreams*. . . . . .

Yet, because of Lucinda's unswerving passion for the tract wrested from the wilderness by Yarbrough and Gerda, the Whetstones still held their land—as a haven to which to come for succor when beset, a shrine on which to lay their trophies in triumph. The family motto was still *Tenebo, I Will Hold*.

And the Whetstones continued as they had for centuries, to build up a domain, to protect therein their own. And, when that stronghold would not suffice in the face of the world's new ways, to hold it as a strong back wall from which to wage a new assault upon a new century. And then, go forth, find, and build anew!

Thus, the strength of Alabama sustains its people even if they leave the state, but the bonds tie them and bring them back to renew that strength. Lella Warren retained her faith in Alabama. The 1941 inscription about the "vigor of Alabama" and "the profession of faith" concludes:

Festival
Participants

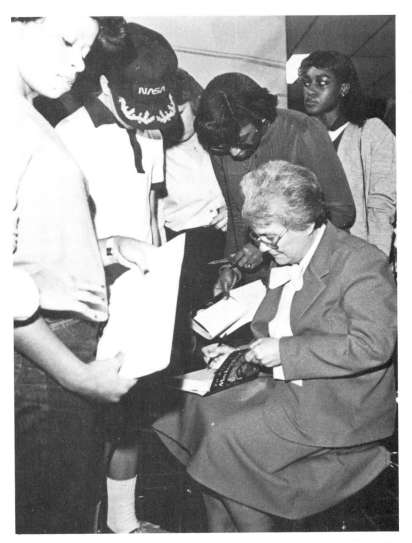

High school students from as far away as Citronelle were among those who came to Eufaula High School to hear Harper Lee speak on the literary quality of Alabama history and to have the Pulitzer Prize-winning author sign copies of To Kill a Mockingbird. *Miss Lee's nephew Hank Conner, a professor of broadcasting at the University of Florida, gave a dramatic reading of Atticus Finch's summation to the jury from the 1960 best-selling novel. (Photo by Bryan Easley)*

"The disposition to be proud and vain of one's country, and to boast of it, is a natural feeling," wrote Joseph Glover Baldwin. The lawyer who came to west Alabama in 1836 was thinking of his native Virginia, not the raw country full of con men, speculators, and homesick vagabonds that inspired him to write Flush Times of Alabama and Mississippi, *now considered one of the major texts of Old Southwest humor. Baldwin left Alabama in 1854 but he was back in Demopolis for the 1983 History and Heritage Festival. His humor was revitalized in a reading by Bert Hitchcock, chairman of Auburn University's English department.* (Photo by Bryan Easley)

A short story told in the voice of a newspaper's country correspondent—and read to an Auburn History and Heritage gathering—tells more about the narrator and her community than the words on newsprint. For Lee Smith, the story entitled "Between the Lines" began when she was editing community correspondence for The Tuscaloosa News. *It won an O. Henry Prize and is published in the author's collection of stories,* Cakewalk. *(Photo by Bryan Easley)*

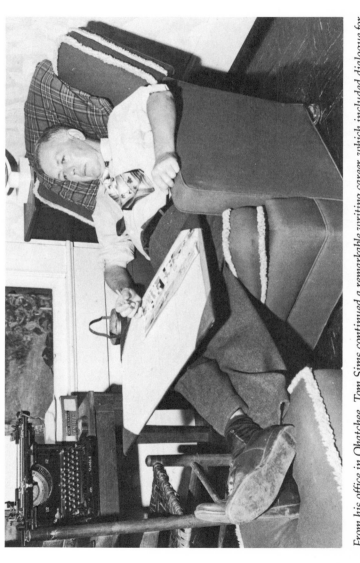

From his office in Ohatchee, Tom Sims continued a remarkable writing career, which included dialogue for comic strips, feature articles, short stories and sketches, and his "Ohatchee USA" column, which ran in newspapers across the country from 1954 until a few years before the writer's death in 1972. Sims started to write in his easy chair and finished at the typewriter shown on the table. John Kelly's introduction to Tom Sims's life and works, emphasizing his return to Alabama, serves in this collection as a prelude to "One to Ohatchee," from The New Yorker *magazine. (Photo courtesy of Jenny Sims Owen)*

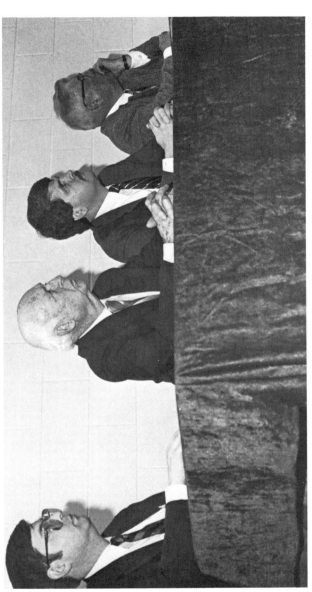

Barbour County's social and political climate has produced several state leaders, among them six of Alabama's forty-eight governors. Appearing before a Eufaula History and Heritage Festival audience, four Barbour Countians, representing prominent political families, explored the southeast Alabama county's traditions and offered personal insights into families, rivalries, and relationships. They are, left to right: Jack Wallace, Jr.; Preston Clayton, a retired associate justice of the Alabama Supreme Court and a former state senator; Charles Blackmon and Robert Flewellen. (Photo by Bryan Easley)

Jim Haskins, the author of more than fifty books and a professor of English at the University of Florida, told History and Heritage Festival audiences in Auburn and Demopolis, his native city, that special conditions in black Alabama communities have produced a marked proportion of successful and nationally prominent people. Haskins related the influences of family, school, and church on his own upbringing in Marengo County. (Photo by Bryan Easley)

In his history of Marengo County's Jewish community, Jacob Koch writes that the county's children have left to make marks for themselves in distant places. These five natives who returned for the Demopolis History and Heritage Festival represent achievement in several areas. They are, left to right, Alan Koch, Jim Haskins, Bert Hitchcock, Raymond Waites, and Bill Cobb. Koch is a Montgomery attorney and a former professional baseball pitcher. Haskins, Hitchcock, and Cobb are writers, scholars, and professors of English. Waites is a New York-based designer and founder of Gear, Inc. The moderator was Dr. Lester Crawford of Gallion, now in Washington, where he is head of the United States Bureau of Veterinary Medicine. (Photo by Bryan Easley)

*As a historian of the modern South and of the Baptist denomination,
Wayne Flynt had the good fortune as a teenager to encounter the legacy of
the Rev. Charles R. Bell, Jr., a former pastor of Parker Memorial Baptist
Church. In his study of Bell's Anniston ministry, Flynt combines the insights of the scholar, the techniques of oral history, and the empathy of a
writer who can see in his subject common influences and related missions.*
(Photo courtesy of Charles R. Bell, Jr. Estate)

Introducing Tom Sims—

American Humorist

JOHN E. KELLY

In many ways, John Kelly represents the ideal amateur humanities student. (An "amateur," let us remind ourselves, performs for love, not simply for pay.) Born a Connecticut Yankee, he earned a B.A. degree in English from Lehigh University in 1939; he was drafted into the Army and came south to Fort McClellan in 1942. He met his wife-to-be in Anniston, and they settled in the city in 1946, after John retired as a captain in the Corps of Engineers. After a successful career in building construction, he started his own materials supply company in 1951. Thirty-two years later he sold it to some of his employees. As active as John Kelly might be in business and civic activities, the work of the humanities has been central to his life. He has served as president of the Alabama Shakespeare Festival and as a member of the Committee for the Humanities in Alabama. His essay introducing Tom Sims's famous *New Yorker* story, adapted from his oral presentation at the Anniston History and Heritage Festival in March 1983, indicates several important scholarly characteristics. More than an affectionate remembrance of an old friend, it places Tom Sims squarely in the tradition of American humor. In this volume John Kelly's work will introduce "The Sage of Ohatchee" to readers who never knew the man who, among his accomplishments, made children try spinach.

MY FRIEND TOM SIMS, now known affectionately as "The Sage of Ohatchee," began his newspaper career when he was six years old, selling *The Birmingham News* and the *Age-Herald*. He first saw those streets when he was three, after his family had moved to the city from Cave Spring, Georgia. His personal enterprise, his energy, and his love of journalism, in evidence so early, never abated through a career spanning five decades. He was a writer of prodigious output. Just how many newspapers he worked for I can't say, but I know he reported for *The Anniston Star* during his summers as an undergraduate at Vanderbilt University. I also know that after he left Vanderbilt and abandoned his plans for a career in law—because, as he told it, pen and paper were lighter than law books—he was a reporter, state editor, copy editor, telegraph editor, and columnist for *The Nashville Tennessean*.

From Nashville, he went to *The Cleveland Press*, where his talents as a humorist gained wider audiences. This was in 1921 and Tom already was a well-educated man and a veteran—of the great war as well as of the newsroom. I suspect that he knew early on that a writer's life was for him. From his liberal arts education at Montgomery Bell Academy in Nashville and at Vanderbilt, he had seen enough of literature to know what he could write and what he wanted to write. He did not stop until shortly before his death at age seventy-four. In the course of a long, active career, he was a reporter, an editorial paragrapher, an essayist, a short-story writer, a dialogue writer for the "Popeye" comic strip for eighteen years, a continuity writer for eight years for the "Amos 'n' Andy" radio show, a staff writer for *Life* magazine, a writer for animated cartoons such as "Tom and Jerry," a free-lancer for publications ranging from *The Saturday Evening Post* to *Progressive Farmer*, and a syndicated columnist.

However, such was the nature of his work that many Alabamians either have never heard of this remarkable writer, or they remember him only as some rustic from near Anniston whose columns, they think, circulated only in state papers. In these remarks introducing one of Tom Sims's most representative stories, I hope to show that he was a writer who put together the general American and the Southern traditions of humor with style and distinction.

I first met Tom Sims about 1946 or 1947 when I settled in Anniston after service in the Army. I have no recollection of our first meeting but I had come to know him mainly through his column, "Ohatchee, USA," which appeared in *The Anniston Star*. Tom smoked a pipe and his red cheeks and cowlick and the twinkle in his eye indicated a state of mind pleasant and appealing. He looked like a department store Santa Claus without the pot belly and false whiskers. He was the sort of man you would speak to in an airport or in the post office, even if you weren't acquainted with him—and people did speak to Tom easily and often. In fact, Tom in person was not noticeably different from Tom in print; it was the same person who showed his optimism and who believed that motivation and a willingness to work would carry a man through.

He had already spent much time in the East, a place I knew, before we came together in Anniston—though I lived in town and, at that time, he lived in the nearby village of Ohatchee, together with his wife Agnes and their two daughters, a mule named Kate, a 999-pound bullfrog (whose size was calculated from the volume of his croak, the actual amphibian never appearing in public), and those other farm animals Tom would write about. However folksy Tom may have appeared, he had learned much about the art of writing while in New York during the thirties, a time when, for people of my generation, that city represented the heyday of the newspaper era.

There were half a dozen flourishing papers there and more outstanding, talented reporters, columnists, drama critics and the like, I believe, than have ever existed in any other time or place. Heywood Broun was writing his marvelous columns; his biblical prose appeared daily in the *World Telegram* and any day might produce a masterpiece. Franklyn P. Adams, author of "The Conning Tower," was a daily delight. Don Marquis's marvelous creation, Archie the Cockroach, was writing his blank verse philosophy and his chronicles of the love life of his sidekick, Mehitabel the Cat. There was also Westbrook Pegler, John Keiran, Alexander Woolcott, and many more. That was the New York Tom Sims lived in, and it must have been an ideal place for a young writer to learn his craft.

Early in his career it began to be obvious that Tom Sims's particular gift was humor. He was the master of the one-liner, and he had gotten some experience with humor when he wrote those editorial paragraphs for the Cleveland newspaper from 1921-1926. Among his other talents as a humorist, he was able to use life-at-the-moment for topical jokes that reflect their own period and at the same time give us some true insight into history. For instance, most of my generation felt the impact of prohibition—the sheer morality of the effort and the immoral consequences. In the larger cities, prohibition created the framework for the organized crime syndicates that have since infiltrated the labor movement and now are running the drug traffic. Tom was aware early on of the farcical enforcement of liquor laws, and his jokes reflected that. "A beer racketeer in New York was buried in a $20,000 mausoleum," he wrote in *Life*, back when it was a humor magazine. "It's a lot of money but the house was on the drinks." And another: " 'I was as sober as the cops who arrested me!' shouted a movie star in a Hollywood court recently. He was convicted due to his weak defense."

Tom Sims's humor revealed a social outrage and a fighting spirit. Like others of our generation, he saw a world war early in his life. In fact, Tom joined the Marines and was wounded in the Argonne Forest in 1918. Following the absurdity of prohibition—which, as Marquis's Archie said, made a man want to cry in his beer and denied him the beer to cry into—Sims was to see the depression, and then, before his death, yet another world war and two "police actions" in Southeast Asia. He wrote, therefore, from a large experience and a large intelligence. In his social commentary, Tom was saying that a social experiment such as prohibition, an attempt to dictate private morality, was bound to be a complete failure; he could see that the attempt to enforce such dictates was both undermining the legal system and corrupting its agents.

From his perspective as a humorist, Tom could write about politics and politicians, but it is not possible to peg him to a party. He apparently found most politicians amply supplied with warts, like all of us, and so his comments aren't violently partisan. Few of the top political figures escaped his humor:

> Calvin Coolidge has rejected an offer to write a weekly article for the Sunday newspaper. We agree with him that the world should shift for itself once a week.

> "Governor Roosevelt has been called fit as a fiddle by physicians," says the *New York Times*. We have noticed that the Tammany chiefs are trying to play on him while the issues burn.

> Plans are underway to "humanize" President Hoover for the American people. A picture of him returning to camp without any fish would help.

From New York Sims could look over the entire country, and he did just that from 1926 to 1941. He had first gone there as a comic-strip continuity writer for King Features Syndicate, a job he got because, according to a 1951 article for *Progressive Farmer*, he always gave a positive answer to any question. (Even if someone asked him to rob a bank, he wrote that his positive answer would be, "Yes, I won't. Yes, I'll stay out of jail.") He wrote the "Popeye" dialogue from 1937 to 1955 for King Features Syndicate. In addition, Tom wrote for "Polly and Her Pals," "Bringing Up Father," "Toots and Casper," and "Tillie the Toiler." In *The Anniston Star*, Tom was quoted as saying that while he lived on Long Island, his hobby was beating Chic Young, the creator of "Blondie," at golf. Sims later took over the strip for a year. Tom also served for three years as an idea man for "Chic" Sale, the comedian whose name became synonymous with outhouse.

Since Tom Sims had such an eye for irony, perhaps the circumstances under which he finally became famous were not lost on him. He found real fame—what is called "name-recognition"—only after he came back home to Alabama, to a place on the Coosa River, the same one he had been born near, across the Georgia line in 1898. His skill, experience, contacts, and reputation came together after 1941, and he was to make the fifty-seven-acre farm and its human and animal inhabitants into household words. His "Ohatchee USA" column ran in papers across the country from 1954 until a few years before his death in 1972.

The Ohatchee years show Tom Sims blossoming into a mature writer who represented the best in the tradition of American and Alabama humor. Obviously he had worked long enough as a professional writer to know what made people laugh. His 999-pound bullfrog is a character everybody who has ever lived in the country or fished around farm ponds knows. If, thinking scientifically, we do try to relate the volume of a frog's croak to its actual size, why not 999 pounds? As the story in *The New Yorker* will show, Tom Sims was so skillful as a writer that he did not have to rely on cheap tricks. But he was also more than a mere craftsman. His finely honed sense of irony—of people and the forces that make them similar and different—joins with his Alabama sense of place and family to create a humor that is enduring. Like Mark Twain, Josh Billings, Bill Nye, Ambrose Bierce, and Mr. Dooley, Tom was a master of styles and techniques. And, like them all, he was something more than the smiling merry man one might meet in the post office. There was mischief in his smile and a hidden irony in that twinkle in his eye.

We get a full view of the subtlety in Tom Sims's humor in *The New Yorker* story. It shows all that I have said and something else: he was not simply a writer who found a quiet place away from the bustle of the East. He was a man who loved his family and this part of the world. He participated in Anniston's civic activities, even to serving as president of the Kiwanis Club. In every sense of the word, he knew what it was like to be from Alabama, and his sure sense of the values involved endears this state to many, even to those born elsewhere, like me.

Much more remains to be said about Tom Sims. I can imagine what a professional biographer might do with the life of a man who wrote so constantly, using so many forms, and, in light of the volume of his work, so well. His ability to make it as a writer without forgetting his roots, and his discipline and care for detail, make him a man whose life and work bear further study. I offer this brief sketch merely as introduction and perhaps to whet the appetite of those who wish to know about an Alabama writer who traveled across America but came back home to a native literary humor that made him famous. I do not want to think of a writer of Tom Sims's merit slipping into oblivion or being thought of as an artist of little consequence. If Alabamians let that happen, then we are not paying proper attention to our history and heritage.

Here then is a story that shows Tom Sims, Alabama writer, at his best.

One to Ohatchee*

TOM SIMS

Sometimes I think that what I look forward to most about a trip to New York is buying a ticket back to my home, in Ohatchee, Alabama. Whenever I do this, some peculiar, haunting little incident is bound to occur. I don't know why, but it always does. Perhaps it's just that the name "Ohatchee" amuses people. At least, that's the conclusion I came to the last time I bought a ticket home. I went to Pennsylvania Station, picked a window and stood in the line before it. When my turn came, the man inside looked out at me. As I remember, he was small and pale, and he wore a green eye shade. "Ohatchee, Alabama," I said to him.

"Ohatchee?" he repeated.

"O-h-a-t-c-h-e-e," I said. "Alabama."

He turned to a large book at his elbow. Confidently at first, and then with assurance ebbing, he flipped the pages back and forth, stopping to pore over several of them. After a while, he peered at me suspiciously. "Ohatchee?" he asked.

"It's a flag stop," I told him.

Tentatively, he glanced at several more pages, and then went out back, through the door of his cage, perhaps to consult another book, an even larger book. After a couple of minutes, he returned, his expression indicating that the expedition had failed. "Ohatchee," he said. He was talking to himself.

"Alabama," I added.

"Are you sure there is such a place?" he asked.

"I live there," I said. "I moved there ten years ago."

"How long ago?"

"Ten years."

"Hmm," he said. He turned again to the book at his elbow.

"My house isn't the only one there," I told him. "Not long ago, one burned down just across the road. People said it had stood there for more than a hundred years. And then, early one morning, it went."

The man behind the window relaxed and smiled faintly. "After a hundred years," he said.

"Yes," I said. "There was a schoolteacher living in a small room upstairs. She jumped out the window onto the roof of a shed without waiting to get her teeth. Later in the day, we raked through the ashes. We found some melted car keys. The fire was too hot for her teeth, I guess, but you could still read the numbers on the keys."

"How did it catch?" asked the man next in line behind me.

"Oil," I said.

I turned my back to the window as I spoke, and I felt guilty, seeing the people in the waiting line. It wasn't any longer than some lines at other windows, but the people at the end seemed more impatient. They had waited longer without moving than the newcomers in the other lines.

"Oil?" the stranger repeated.

"Yes," I told him. "Coal oil. Some people call it kerosene. It can be very dangerous in a glass jug."

"Glass jug?" he said.

"The man who owned the house got up before day to build a fire in the grate," I told him. "He poured oil from a glass jug on the kindling, and then he must have bumped the jug and cracked it when he set it on the cement hearth. After he lit the kindling, he went out in the yard. Pretty soon, he smelled something like cloth burning and went back inside. A big rug in front of the fireplace was a solid blaze."

"No fire extinguisher?" the stranger asked.

"Nothing but water," I said.

"Water will spread an oil fire," he said.

"They didn't get much chance to see if it would, because about that time the man's grandfather came running out of his bedroom, yelling. The old man always slept in his long undershirt, and that's all he was wearing—not even drawers."

"So the man had to rescue his grandfather," said the stranger.

"No," I said. "The man went out to the back porch and pushed a button that turned on the new electric water pump. The house had stood a hundred years without any fire protection, and only a few weeks before, they'd wired it for electricity and had thrown away the well bucket. The new pump hit about six licks and stopped dead."

"Wouldn't start again?" asked the stranger.

"It couldn't," I said. "No electricity. The grandfather was more afraid of electricity than he was of the fire. The first thing he did was to make for the kitchen and pull the switch that cut off all the current. That left the house burning and no water. The well bucket was gone, and the well itself had been sealed over when they put the pump in. Someone blew the sawmill whistle, and people came with tubs of water, but by then it was too late. The fire had gone up through the walls, and the schoolteacher had jumped from upstairs without her teeth."

The man suddenly glanced at the big station clock and then checked it with his watch. He hurried away, and I saw him take his place at the end of another line. Most of the people in my line had already gone elsewhere, and now the remaining ones went. I turned again to the man behind the ticket window. He was using his phone, which he cradled between his shoulder and his chin, leaving his hands free to fumble abstractedly with the book. Evidently, he had exhausted all his near-at-hand resources, and was calling someone with access to more abstruse information. There was a long pause. The man and I waited patiently. A strange look came on his face. He hunched his shoulder to bring the phone closer to his ear. "Are you *sure*?" he asked.

There was another pause. "O.K.," he said. "If you say so."

He hung up and frowned at me. "I still don't believe it," he said.

He opened the book to a page near the back and ran his finger up and down it. Eventually the finger stopped and the man slowly lifted his head and looked at me. He seemed dazed but obliged to abide by what he had found there. He reached for a ticket and inspected it for length. Apparently, it wasn't long enough. He selected another and reluctantly took his pen in hand. "Ohatchee," he said with disapproval as he began writing.

"O-h-a-t-c-h-e-e," I said.

I was tempted to apologize to him. Sometimes, finding myself in one of the queer situations the name of my town gets me into, I have considered moving my family to Cleveland or St. Louis or some other known place, but my wife and I have two children, and they have a mule, a pony, two goats, four dogs, three cats, and twelve ducks. None of us would want to leave any of these behind.

"Ohatchee," the man repeated to himself as he continued writing. He had reached the last section of the ticket. "Ohatchee, Alabama," he muttered. "I never heard of the place."

"It's nice there," I told him.

"I never heard of it," he said.

Barbour County:

Home of Governors

ROBERT FLEWELLEN

AND CHARLES BLACKMON

To an outsider, Barbour County politics might appear to be an impenetrable thicket in its own right, but to the two authors of this essay it is a set of complex and overlapping trails—the kind historians like to follow. Although in this essay, the personal pronoun "I" is suppressed and replaced with an implied "we," each writer speaks with individual authority. Robert Flewellen holds an A.B. in English and an M.A. in history from the University of Alabama; he taught history for thirty years in the public schools. He is also the nephew of Governor Chauncey Sparks. Charles Blackmon is an accountant with a University of Virginia degree. He is the son of Alice Shorter Comer Blackmon, the two middle names providing a clue to two gubernatorial connections. His great-grandfather was Governor William D. Jelks. The two au-

thors grew up hearing the stories of blood-kin, friendships, political differences, and state campaigns. Close to home, they understand Barbour County's unique political climate—a melodramatic arrangement of populism and elitism, city and county, with these differences more often a matter of political style than a reflection of personal status. The county has been, and may still be, an ideal proving ground for state political efforts. Alabama historians who attended the Eufaula History and Heritage Festival in March 1983 found something new to deliberate in the presentation of the two men. What they offer is a particular view of a Faulknerian world, about which more will certainly be written in the future.

BARBOUR COUNTY IS OFTEN CALLED the "Home of Governors," and rightly so. In the 164 years since Alabama entered the Union in December 1819 as the twenty-second state, forty-eight persons have served as chief executive. If these governors had been shared equally on a county basis, each of the sixty-seven counties could claim about three-fourths of a governor. But Barbour claims six of the forty-eight who were either born in the county or claimed the county as home: John Gill Shorter, William Dorsey Jelks, Braxton Bragg Comer, Chauncey Sparks, George Corley Wallace, and Lurleen Burns Wallace. These six governors have served, at this writing, more than thirty years. Such a record adds credence to the old political saying remembered from high school days: "Alabama is divided into three parts—North Alabama, South Alabama, and Barbour County."

The six-governor record may be even more remarkable in light of the in-county political jealousies that have existed for many years between residents of Eufaula (located on the eastern edge of the county and today containing slightly over fifty percent of the county's population) and residents of Clayton (the county seat, located in the geographic center of the county). The county maintains two county courthouses—one in Eufaula, one in Clayton—and political races for county offices are often hotly contested. Campaigns are waged and candidates chosen with the Eufaula-Clayton rivalry never far out of mind. Yet the county has remained united in supporting her native or adopted sons and daughter who have sought the state's highest political office. The record speaks for itself—whether the candidates be from Eufaula, Clayton, or Clio.

Barbour Countians are mindful of their six governors and of the impact of their gubernatorial records that encompass a time frame of 125 years of Alabama history. In the following survey of their careers, much that is stated might be familiar to many, but the information will introduce new readers to this company of distinguished politicians. The survey may also present some historical facts not so well-known, namely the interconnections of families that yielded what might be described as a minor dynasty. The survey and the discussions of family connections may further show that local history can contain unpublished details that illuminate the careers of noted leaders such as these six men.

The first, John Gill Shorter, was inaugurated in 1861; he was born and educated in Georgia, but for fifty-four years was an Alabama citizen and a resident of Eufaula, where he practiced law. He served in the Alabama legislature in both the House and the Senate and was a circuit judge. A member of the Alabama Secession Convention, he represented Alabama at the Georgia Secession Convention. During his two years as governor, his energies were consumed by the war effort—providing for the families of men serving in the Confederate armies and building the military defenses of the City of Mobile.

William Dorsey Jelks served as governor for five years and eight months, beginning in 1901. A portion of his tenure was as acting governor due to the illness and death of Governor William J. Samford. Jelks was then elected to a four-year term of his own, taking office in 1902. Born in Macon County, Alabama, and a resident of Union Springs, Jelks was educated at Mercer University in Macon, Georgia. Moving to Eufaula, he managed a local newspaper, *The Eufaula Times*. Under his leadership, this paper was widely quoted throughout the state and "claimed a larger circulation than any other Alabama newspaper," according to Charles G. Summersell's *Alabama History for Schools*. In Eufaula, Jelks served on the local school board and for a time was superintendent of schools. He also represented Barbour County in the state Senate and served as president of that body. As governor he was known as a friend of education, an opponent of child labor, and an advocate of efficiency and economy in state government. He later organized and served as the first president of the Protective Life Insurance Company of Birmingham.

Braxton Bragg Comer, one of Alabama's most important governors, was inaugurated on 14 January 1907. A native of Barbour County, he was born at Old Spring Hill and was a student at the University of Alabama when the federal troops, Croxton's Raiders, burned many of the university buildings. Comer received B.A. and M.A. degrees at the University of Georgia and Emory and Henry College in Virginia. His administration as governor was noted for farsighted improvements in education and in the regulation of railroads. Governor Comer was a pioneer in urging state conservation laws, in measures prohibiting child labor for those under twelve years of age, and he was instrumental in establishing a tuberculosis sanitarium. In his many business successes he was probably best known as president of Avondale Mills. In 1920 he was appointed U.S. Senator.

Chauncey Sparks, Alabama's chief executive beginning in 1943, was born in Barbour County 8 October 1884. He was educated at Mercer University where he was awarded the A.B. and LL.B. degrees. He returned to Eufaula in 1910 to practice law. Sparks served as judge of the Inferior Court, Precinct 5, Barbour County, for five years and was a member of the state legislature (1919-1923 and 1931-1939). His administration was noted for aid to education, the establishment of the Medical College in Birmingham, building the "farm to market" roads, and the fight against discriminatory freight rates. Under his leadership the state debt was reduced by twenty-five percent.

Louise Sparks Flewellen is an only sister of "Uncle Chan," as all of his nephews and nieces called him, and she and her children lived for many years in the governor's Eufaula home with the governor, a lifelong bachelor. (The home was built in 1856 and is listed in the National Register of Historic Places.)

He is remembered as an honest, hard-working person, a man of the highest integrity. He had a brilliant mind and an almost photographic memory. Frugal in his personal habits, he was a "gentleman farmer" of sorts and was an entertaining conversationalist. He was also temperamental. On occasion he could be a sullen and moody person. He enjoyed "playing jokes" but was not very good at taking a joke. But in his own way he loved his family and was loyal to them. Enjoying both hunting and fishing, he was an expert angler but a poor marksman. He cherished the land and streams of Alabama and was undeniably a countryman at heart.

George Corley Wallace, a native of Clio but a resident of Clayton for many years, was first inaugurated governor of Alabama in January 1963. He was educated at the University of Alabama, where he was awarded a degree in law, and served in the United States Air Force during World War II. Prior to becoming governor, he served as assistant attorney general for the state, appointed to that post by Governor Sparks. (A protégé of Sparks, Wallace was a frequent visitor to Governor Sparks's Eufaula law offices.) Wallace was a member of the Alabama House of Representatives and was elected circuit judge of the Third Judicial Circuit of Alabama. He was first inaugurated governor in 1963, again in 1971, the third time in 1975, and began an unprecedented fourth term on 17 January 1983. His administrations have been noted for promoting education, building new trade schools and junior colleges, road building, and attracting new industries to Alabama.

Wallace's father, a farmer, was active in county government. At the time of his death, he was chairman of the Barbour County Board of Revenue. His mother worked for twenty-two years in the State Health Department, and his grandfather, a country doctor, was at one time probate judge of Barbour County.

George Wallace grew up in Clio during the Great Depression. He and his family were "poor" in the same sense that most other families in Barbour County were "poor" during the 1930s. Against the background of the Great Depression, he had a reputation of being a hard worker and a fighter; his Golden Gloves championship lent credence to his moniker "the fighting judge." An advocate of states rights—yet a racist in the minds of many—George Wallace held a unique appeal to a broad spectrum of voters at both the state and national level. (He polled ten million votes in 1968 as presidential candidate of the American Independent Party.)

Lurleen Burns Wallace, wife of George C. Wallace, was inaugurated governor of Alabama in January 1967. Mrs. Wallace had the distinction of being the only woman to serve as governor of Alabama. She was a native of Tuscaloosa County, but Barbour claimed her as an adopted daughter. She was elected governor on the basis of her husband's previous record and popularity with Alabama voters, and at a time when the state constitution prohibited a governor from succeeding himself. The Wallace program was continued during her administration, a term cut tragically short by a losing fight with cancer. Governor Wallace died of cancer on 7 May 1968, but she had won the support and admiration of Alabamians.

These, then, were the six—Shorter, Jelks, Comer, Sparks, Wallace, and Wallace. But why so many from rural Barbour County in the southeast quadrant of the state, a county whose population has never been in excess of 25,000 persons? Several factors may have contributed to the election of these six governors. All were well-educated; five were college graduates (Lurleen Wallace was a graduate of Tuscaloosa County High School and had attended a business school). Five of the six were professional and business people: Shorter, Sparks, and George Wallace were lawyers; Jelks was a well-known newspaper man; Comer was a banker and president of Avondale Mills.

Four of the six had held other state and public offices, providing a background of experience and a knowledge of state politics, both valuable assets when seeking the governor's chair. Shorter was a member of the Alabama House and Senate and was a circuit judge; Jelks was president of the Alabama Senate; Sparks was a court judge and member of the Alabama House; George Wallace was an assistant attorney general, a member of the Alabama House, and a circuit judge.

However, in recapping such facts, the role that family connections and friendships played cannot be ignored, although few historians appear to have noticed. The family chart following this narrative will help clarify this discussion of the family ties of three of the Barbour County governors: Shorter, Jelks, and Comer.

John Gill Shorter, the Civil War governor, was elected when secession was creating tremendous emotional stress. At that time, Barbour County was one of the larger, more cultural counties of the state, and the Shorter name was storied during this era. One of Governor Shorter's brothers, Henry R. Shorter, was well known in the state and served as president of the Railroad Commission in 1890. This was a very influential position at that time and, as we gather from other information about Governors Jelks and Comer, railroad rates were a big issue during their terms of office, which began only ten years after Henry R. Shorter served his term as head of the Railroad Commission.

Governor Jelks's connection is to Henry R. Shorter. William Dorsey Jelks moved to Eufaula and purchased the *Times and News* in September of 1880. On 7 June 1884, he married Alice Keitt Shorter, the daughter of Henry R. Shorter. As we know, Jelks was a capable newspaper man from 1880 until 1898 when he sold his interest, but did having a wife whose uncle was governor and whose father was involved in what was probably the key issue of the day hurt or help his career? Obviously the answer is that it helped. Is it possible that Jelks would have been just a successful businessman, never entering politics, without these family connections? Of course one can only speculate, but certainly that is a possibility. Other Shorter family members served in politics including a first cousin of Alice's: Clement Clay Shorter was speaker of the Alabama House of Representatives at age twenty-six.

The family connections between the Shorter and Jelks families are also connected to Braxton Bragg Comer. Governor Comer's life is well documented, and it would be difficult to prove that his connections to the Shorter and Jelks lines were the most important link to his political career, especially considering the political differences between Jelks and Comer. However, his blood ties to politics undoubtedly had some influence in his life.

From their Barbour County farm the six Comer brothers all became successful men, with three of them becoming millionaires. One of the closest brothers to Braxton Bragg Comer was St. George Legaré Comer. They were close in age and attended school together. The often-told tale of B. B. Comer walking home to Barbour County from the University of Alabama during the Civil War surely created a strong bond between them, as it was George who accompanied him on that trip.

The Shorter-Jelks-Comer connection is complex and politically significant. St. George Legaré Comer married Laura Thornton, the daughter of Mary Shorter and Dr. William H. Thornton, and the granddaughter of none other than Governor John Gill Shorter. One of their sons, Edward Trippe Comer II, married his third cousin, Catherine Shorter Jelks, the only child of Alice Shorter and Governor William D. Jelks. This family tie may not be quite as direct as the Shorter-to-Jelks relationship, but it nonetheless indicates a strong intertwining of families at a time when family ties were quite influential.

A short story here might further expand on this idea of family camaraderie. The following is an excerpt from a story told by Dr. Edward T. Comer to David Alsobrook while Alsobrook was researching his master's thesis on William Dorsey Jelks. Dr. Edward T. Comer is the grandson of Jelks and of St. George L. Comer.

> One time I asked Grandpa [Jelks]: "Grandpa, how come Uncle Bragg [B. B. Comer] doesn't like you?" And he said, "Son, I'm going to explain something to you about politics. Uncle Bragg is very fond of me, I think, and certainly I am of him, and by the way, he wants you to come up and see him." So I got on my shoes and socks and walked up there about two blocks. "Bigpa" had already talked to Uncle Bragg and told him I was coming. . . . He was trying to say to me that what people say in politics or is printed in papers does not always mean any personal animosity at all. It's a political feeling, a thought.

Dr. Comer's sister, Alice Comer Blackmon, recalls visiting her grandfather, George L. Comer, often for Sunday lunch when she was a girl. After lunch the men would gather for talk, which naturally would have included politics. George Comer was a mayor of Eufaula, and surely this Sunday-lunch tradition had been carried on for some time.

These two stories lend personal credence to the theory of family ties possibly being a catalyst in the rise of these three men to the top position in our state—John Shorter and William Jelks through their blood ties and B. B. Comer through his close relationship with his brother, George, and his family. Obviously, they were well qualified in their own right, but "Why did they seek office?" and "Why were they elected over men who were also well qualified?" Could it be that the family background and interrelationships were something "extra" that helped them succeed where others failed?

Lurleen Wallace was elected on her husband's political reputation. Governor Sparks was friend to young George Wallace and helped "get him started" in state office and state politics. Circuit Judge Jack Wallace is a brother of George. Campaign manager for Sparks was his younger brother, Leon A. Sparks, who had an established business reputation in an Eufaula-based insurance partnership with their brother, Hugh C. Sparks. Leon Sparks knew businessmen across the state and had a "politician's personality"—an extrovert, a man who could smile and shake hands easily with voters from all walks, and a tireless worker. More than any other person, Leon Sparks may have been responsible for the election of Chauncey Sparks.

From Shorter to the Wallaces, Barbour County has fostered governors. The two poles of aristocracy and populism existed in the county, and in that environment a tradition of family support and political interdependency played an important role. A power base existed in Barbour, supported by blood and friendship as much as by political issues. It is also worth noting that, in addition to its governors, Barbour has, for years, displayed an influence far greater than its agricultural county status. For example, of the 36 senators and 105 representatives making up the state legislature, Barbour claimed one senator and two representatives for years—a political strength out of proportion to the county's rural population. The political force of Barbour County has been felt in the successful careers of other prominent office-holders, among them Reuben Kolb, Charles McDowell, Jere Beasley, Jack Wallace, James Clark, and Preston Clayton.

As a coda, to explain the myriad connections that existed among three families alone, and perhaps to encourage other students who wish to explore the ties of kinship that suggest political bonds, the following diagram and some remarks on a few of the principals is offered.

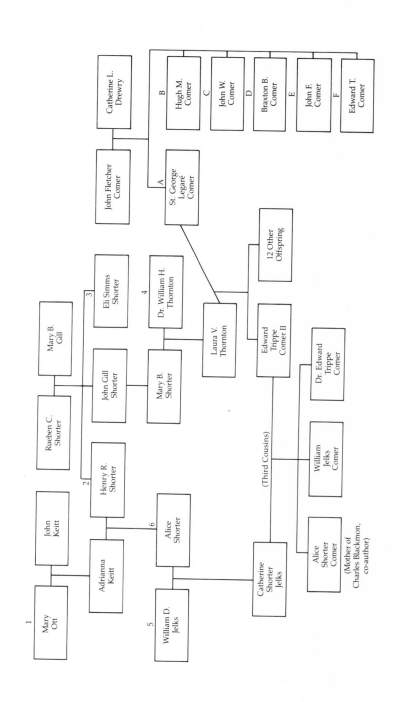

1. Early widowed. Married Benjamin Treadwell. Built "Big House" on The Hill known as the "Jelks House." Demolished 1964. Mrs. Treadwell strong woman during the war. See *Backtracking in Barbour County*.

2. President of the Alabama Railroad Commission in 1890. One of the best known men in Alabama at the time.

3. Representative in National Congress before the war. His son built "Shorter Mansion."

4. First mayor of Eufaula.

5. His father was killed in the Civil War. Traces ancestry to the Cromwells of England.

6. Remarkable woman in her own right. John Gill Shorter was her uncle as was Eli Sims Shorter. Clement Clay Shorter, speaker of Alabama House at age 26, was her cousin. The book *Backtracking in Barbour County* was dedicated to her.

A. Noted Eufaula & Alabama attorney and mayor of Eufaula for over ten years.

B. President of Georgia Central Railroad and Ocean Steamship Company.

C. Georgia planter and vice-president of Cowikee Mills.

D. Governor, senator, and head of Avondale Mills.

E. Planter and postmaster.

F. President of Bibb Manufacturing Company

The Humanistic

Black Heritage

of Alabama

JIM HASKINS

A standard resumé might tell a reader that James S. Haskins, a native of Demopolis, is professor of English at the University of Florida and author of more than fifty books for both the adult trade and young adult audiences. The resumé would not say that he derived his values in a region named for both his skin color and the color of the soil. Coming back to Alabama for the History and Heritage Festival, Jim Haskins could assume a position in his fortieth year that would not have been a possibility twenty years earlier. He is not merely a successful black Alabamian, he is one of the most prolific writers in the country, and his journey has been accompanied by advanced academic degrees and honors. A member of Phi Beta Kappa, he holds degrees from Georgetown University and the University of New Mexico. He was in Alabama during the civil rights struggle, and his travels across the country since then have given him a perspective on that period and on this state. His remarks on the black humanistic tradition, delivered before both an Auburn and a Demopolis audience, are directed to Alabamians black and white. Transcending but not ignoring the questions of race, the words call attention to the human code of personal accountability which is central to Jim Haskins's life and work. He is able to examine the character and integrity of athletes, singers, teachers, poets, authors, and diplomats because of the basic human lessons he learned in the Black Belt and never forgot. His latest book is *Bricktop*, which he co-authored with the famous nightclub hostess who went by that name.

THERE IS SOMETHING about growing up black in Alabama that has historically encouraged one to strive for excellence. This is a thesis I began to develop after I left Alabama, after I had gone to school in Boston and Georgetown and Albuquerque, and then settled in New York City. Over the years, in these various places, I met many other blacks from Alabama. The majority of them, it seemed to me, were either already successful or soon intended to be. Attempting to document that thesis was something I wanted to do when I had the time, and I remember feeling somewhat taken aback when I learned that Horace Mann Bond had already done so. In the 1950s he had documented the geographical origins of black professionals and holders of Ph.D. degrees and found that a substantial number had roots in Alabama and that, of these, an extremely high percentage traced their roots to Perry County.

Originally published in his book, *The Nation's Children*, in 1960, this material was later included in a U.S. Office of Education study that Bond did in 1967. Andrew Billingsley also cited Bond's research in his widely read *Black Families in White America*, published in 1968. Horace Mann Bond, for those who are not familiar with his name, was the foremost black educator of his time. He served as president of both Fort Valley State College in Georgia and Lincoln University in Pennsylvania, taught at a variety of other colleges, and devoted his life to furthering black education. He was the father of Georgia State Senator Julian Bond.

One of his many research projects was to investigate the sources of achievement of black professionals. In going through the biographies of 400 to 500 successful men and women, he found that the majority of all black Ph.D. holders, physicians, and college teachers were descended from fewer than 500 extended families in existence in 1860. He also found that the approximately ten percent of the blacks who were free in 1860 dominated the subsequent production of black professionals and intellectuals. He once wrote that he believed these findings to be "an eloquent testimonial to what advantages accrue from somebody in the early history of the family getting a break, in terms of money and education." Seeking to explain this phenomenon further, Dr. Bond posited that strong-willed parents with high aspirations for their children—and a good school—were additional elements that worked in conjunction with a family history of literacy and freedom to produce men and women of distinction.

Andrew Billingsley took the exploration a step further. Through discussions with Dr. Bond, he extended the roots of black excellence to include the community, which was a source of support for the black family and must, therefore, at least indirectly, influence men and women of distinction. Billingsley defined the supports at the community level as a good school, the church, and an intellectual atmosphere in the community. In *Black Families in White America*, he illustrated this thesis with a study of Marion, Alabama, which happens to be in Perry County. Billingsley was born and spent his first seven years there. Of the various community supports, the presence in Marion of the Lincoln Normal School seemed to go farthest in explaining why so many black Ph.D.'s hailed from Perry County.

Horace Mann Bond coined an interesting phrase to describe the interacting elements of family and community as they work to produce men and women of distinction. He called it an "ecology of academic excellence." When Bond coined this phrase, the word *ecology* was not associated in the public mind so specifically with the earth's resources as it is today. He employed the word in its larger meaning: the system of relationships between organisms and their environments. His specific reference, of course, was to human organisms.

At any rate, although I was pleased to find some confirmation of my own theory, I had thought it an original idea. However, it soon occurred to me that both Bond and Billingsley were primarily interested in professionals and academicians. My interest was, and always has been, more wide-ranging. Certainly, I am interested in all black intellectuals who hail from Alabama. To name just a few, in addition to Billingsley:

- John Henrik Clarke, distinguished scholar and author or editor of nearly a dozen books. He was born in Union Springs.
- C. Eric Lincoln, scholar and educator, first president of the Black Academy of Arts and Letters; first black editor of a major series under the imprint of a major publisher (the black religion series issued by Doubleday that bears his name). His birthplace was Athens.
- Marva Collins, the only black educator in history to have a TV movie made about her, and whose role was played by none other than Cicely Tyson. Marva Collins was born in Monroeville.

Also like Bond and Billingsley, I take pride in the fact that Dr. Percy Julian hails from Alabama. He was born in Montgomery. Among his 105 medical patents are his process for synthesizing the female hormone, progesterone, and his process for synthesizing cortisone. Since I suffer from an allergy and must be treated with cortisone when a reaction occurs, I am particularly indebted to Dr. Julian for making cortisone widely available at low cost. Over the years, I have met many other physicians who were born in Alabama. Percy Julian is merely the most famous.

There are other people of distinction who do not fall into the categories that most concerned Bond and Billingsley. My interest includes people who were in the forefront of the civil rights movement: The Rev. Ralph David Abernathy, born in Linden; the Rev. Fred L. Shuttlesworth, a native of Montgomery; Coretta Scott King, born in Marion; and of course, Rosa Parks, who sparked the Montgomery bus boycott, which in turn sparked the civil rights movement. She was born in Tuskegee.

My list of men and women of distinction would have to include political figures like Mayor Kenneth Gibson of Newark, who was born in Enterprise, and Mayor Coleman Young of Detroit, who was born in Tuscaloosa; and military figures like Brig. Gen. Oliver W.

Dillard, who was the first black to achieve this rank in the army. Margaret, Alabama, was his birthplace. Also, people who, when cast into the limelight, proved worthy of it, like Mrs. Andrew Young, who was born in Marion.

I have always included "professionals" in a much broader sense than either Horace Bond or Andrew Billingsley talked about. Professional entertainers, for example: Erskine Hawkins, a native of Birmingham, who composed "Tuxedo Junction"; Big Mama Thornton, born Willie Mae in Montgomery; and Lionel Hampton, born in Birmingham. Professional athletes: Jesse Owens, a native of Danville; Willie Mays, born in Westfield; Hank Aaron, whose birthplace was Mobile; and, most importantly, Joe Louis, the "Brown Bomber," who was born in Lexington.

Some day I would like to research the lives of these and other black men and women of distinction, with a view toward establishing a different kind of "ecology." Much broader than Horace Bond's "ecology of academic excellence," it would be an "ecology of *human* excellence."

I know some might think that *human* is too general a category— too much of an automatic "given"—to have much meaning. But to blacks like myself, who were born before World War II, the word *human* has a very important meaning. It was not for me, nor for the other people whose names I have just listed, a quality or a state of being that could be taken for granted at all. For the major part of our history here in America, we black people have not been accorded by our fellow inhabitants of this continent full membership in the human race.

Come to think of it, what does it mean to be human? Mulling that question over, I am struck by the fact that the state of being human has a variety of references and meanings. In the biological sense, the term *human* has a fairly specific reference. A biological human being walks upright, has a certain-sized brain, is capable of thought, and communicates by means of spoken language. But even the biological definition of a human being is somewhat cloudy—witness the conflict over the issue of abortion. The definition of a human being becomes even more clouded when the concept of culture is introduced. In a very real sense, a human being is defined by the culture into which he or she happens to be born, or into which he or she happens to be transported.

In African culture, for example, a man or woman could claim full membership in the human race and still be captured and enslaved. Most of the slaves who were brought to the new world from Africa were sold to white slavers by their fellow Africans. When the slaves arrived in America, however, they faced an additional change in status. In America, whose culture was based on the Judaeo-Christian ethic, slavery and the state of "human beinghood" could not coexist. The African slaves were thus declared property and the historical record is replete with documentation that slaves were dealt with in the same way as . . . horses. They were "bred" like horses, bought and sold like horses, and were entitled to the same legal rights as horses—which is to say, none at all.

When the Emancipation Proclamation declared the slaves free, it also elevated them to the status of human beings. Thus, the bloodline of an original slave from Africa was reinstated to human beinghood by the very culture that had denied it in the first place.

The freeing of the slaves was an abrupt action. The legal, economic, and psychological mechanisms that had been developed to rationalize the coexistence of two peoples who were biologically but not legally the same could not be nullified with the mere flourish of a quill pen. The majority culture was so threatened by the change that it flatly resisted. Indeed, the American majority is still grappling with this problem.

In the national mind, and especially in the mind of the South, where former slaves who had become human beings actually lived, the radical change in the status of blacks mandated by the Emancipation Proclamation did not actually occur. Blacks were not elevated from slavery to full human beinghood. Rather, their status was raised slightly to a limbo-like state best described by the term *sub-human*. This term was fairly popular in racist circles before the civil rights movement and, in some quarters, enjoys favor still.

Without belaboring the point further, I will simply state that the people whom Horace Bond studied, and the majority of the "famous blacks from Alabama" whom I listed earlier, not to mention all the black Alabamians born before World War II who did not become lettered or famous but who tried to live good lives and to make life better for their children—all these people had a barrier to get past that no white Alabamian ever had to consider: they had to define their *own* humanity. For them, humanity was not a given, and it was not willingly accorded them by the larger culture. Humanity, in the philosophical sense, was something that they had to create for themselves.

On the most basic level, it is this historic ability to define our own humanity, and thereby to create a heritage of which we can be proud, that to me is the most significant aspect of being a black Alabamian. In a way, the very majority culture that denied full humanity to blacks for so long also presented us with one of the means to define it ourselves. I am thinking, of course, about the church.

Although the Judaeo-Christian ethic, as defined by Americans, managed to accommodate slavery, it could not accommodate the presence of slaves who were also "heathens." Christianity was brought to us, and we not only accepted it but adopted it fully. Especially its precepts about suffering here on earth in order to ensure a better life in the hereafter and about turning the other cheek. In fact, by taking such Christian teachings so thoroughly to heart, we outdid a lot of the white folks who had brought them to us. As a people, we were not innately better than whites. That we believed so completely in the concept of Christian humility reflected the reality of our legal existence. That we so patiently waited for our "Promised Land" was primarily a function of having nowhere to go *but* up. Still, that deep religiosity had a way of pervading our lives and of giving root to a humanitarianism of which I feel blacks should be especially proud. Blacks, as a people, did not have to define their humanity by deeming anyone else sub-human. They did not need a negative foil to establish their own identity.

At least that was how I was brought up. The humanitarian philosophy with which I was imbued as a child encouraged the idea of *helping* others, not bringing them down. And I have an idea that other black Alabamians were raised on a similar philosophy. To refer briefly to my list of important black Alabamians: Marva Collins became famous because she believed that "unteachable children" could be taught. Big Mama Thornton has spent a good portion of her career as a blues singer giving free concerts in prisons. Lionel

Hampton has used part of his fortune to build low-cost housing for poor people. Joe Louis, during the World War II years, risked his heavyweight title twice and in both instances donated his winning purses to charity. Of course, none of these people, indeed, no one at all, can define his or her own humanity alone. Everyone needs the support of the surrounding environment.

In recent years, the vogue among some white sociologists and other "experts" in related fields has been to describe the black family as fragmented, and the segregated black church and community as productive of the abnormal. But these "experts" are short-sighted and insufficiently cognizant of the adaptive mechanisms of human beings—in this case, black human beings. Listen to Horace Mann Bond's criteria for his "ecology of academic excellence" and try not to think in terms of a specific race: (1) a history of family literacy; (2) a strong-willed father; (3) a loving mother with strong aspirations for her children; and (4) a good school. With a color-blind still on your mind's eye, listen to Andrew Billingsley's list of elements of community support for family life: (1) a good school; (2) the church; and (3) an intellectual atmosphere in the community. Are not these same elements necessary for academic excellence in people of any race? And what is it about the Alabama environment that has historically provided the necessary combination of these elements to produce a marked proportion of black achievers?

When you broaden the standards of excellence, as I have, to include non-academics, attempts to explain what is so unique about Alabama are even more difficult. My list of famous Alabamians includes people who have had very little formal education, people who did not have strong-willed fathers, people who are not particularly religious. Being born in Alabama, however, gave them some kind of incentive, some combination of the various support elements, some elusive "ecology of human excellence" that encouraged them to succeed.

As I have said, some day I would like to try to track down that elusive key, or combination of elements. For the time being, however, I can only write knowledgeably about myself and about the elements of my growing up in Alabama that encouraged my striving for excellence.

Like Bond and Billingsley, I think first of the family. What my family and other black families in Demopolis imbued in their children was a firm belief that the social and legal distinctions between whites and blacks were not divinely ordained. I was taught that whites were privileged people who, in many instances, enjoyed unfair privileges. But I was never taught to perceive even the most racist of whites as other than misguided. These teachings on the part of my parents derived partly from church teachings. They also derived from association with whites: black women genuinely loved the white children they cared for. Some white women were genuinely concerned about the black women who worked for them.

One of the white women for whom my mother worked gave me the opportunity to read books from the Demopolis Public Library. When I was growing up, black people could not patronize the library. When my mother told this white woman about my voracious desire to read, she volunteered to check books out of the library for me. If not for her, I might have continued to have, as my primary reading aside from books I got at school, only the family encyclopedia. It wasn't bad reading, mind you, but it was a bit dry. Even if I had not been able to read books from the Demopolis Public Library, that would have been no excuse for illiteracy. I had the encyclopedia, after all. As a matter of fact, any excuses that involved blaming whites, or racism, or segregation, got short shrift in my family, and my family was not unique.

Albert Murray, a writer who lives in New York, wrote a book called *South to a Very Old Place*, published in 1971. The book is essentially a chronicle of his return visit to his homeplace—Mobile—by way of New Haven, Connecticut, Greensboro, North Carolina, Atlanta, and Tuskegee. Remembering what he was taught as a child growing up in Mobile, Murray wrote:

> Absolutely the last thing in the world you could ever imagine yourself . . . doing was coming back complaining, "Look what they did to me," . . . because the only one you could possibly blame anything on, even when you did run afoul of white viciousness, was yourself. Absolutely the only thing you could possibly come back saying even then was: "I'm the one. That's all right about them. It's me." Because I already knew exactly what to expect and I still

didn't do what I was supposed to do when the time came . . . that time. But that was that time, watch me next time.

My parents taught me the same thing: if you go out into the world, you better know how to behave in that world. No excuses for messing up. And my parents were not just talking about the world of Demopolis.

They were keenly interested in the world outside Demopolis, and particularly in the achievements of other black Americans in the outside world. They read *Ebony* and *Jet* and the *Pittsburgh Courier*, which purported to be the key "to understanding the progress of the race." Among the grownups, blacks who made it were a common topic of discussion. Demopolis was light-years away from the great cities of Europe, and the lives of my parents were equally as alien to the lives of cosmopolitan black entertainers like Josephine Baker and Bricktop. But it was a peculiar fact of existence for the average, aware black resident of Demopolis to be on intimate terms with the stories of those American blacks who had managed to achieve fame. My parents talked about Josephine Baker and Bricktop and Jackie Robinson and Ralph Bunche as familiarly as they talked about Cousin Eliza and Aunt Cindy.

What this kind of talk established in the mind of a small boy was not only a sense of horizons far beyond those of Demopolis but also the idea that stars were people who were not essentially different from Cousin Eliza and Aunt Cindy.

I also attended an excellent school. It was segregated, of course. My classmates and my teachers were all black. My school did not have up-to-date textbooks, nor much equipment for extracurricular activities like music and sports. But it had superb teachers. Back then, when so many other professions were closed to blacks, teaching was a highly respected, even exalted, profession. In fact, when some other professions began to open up to blacks, older folks just couldn't relate to their children who pursued these different fields.

I have an editor-friend, about my age, whose mother could not understand why she would choose to become an editor at a publishing house. "But what is that you *do*?" the mother always wanted to know. My friend says she finally got herself off the hook when she started teaching an evening course at a local college. Thereafter, her mother would proudly introduce her as a teacher, at such-and-such college, and never mention the fact that her daughter spent most of her time as an editor.

My teachers enjoyed the community support they received. They also earned it. For them, teaching was a true vocation, and it did not stop when school hours were over. When they traveled, they shared their experiences with us, brought back books for us. They did independent research on subjects they believed were important to us—black history, for example. It was not on the official Demopolis public school curriculum, but it was taught in my school. Not only did we learn about the lives of famous blacks in history, but most of the time their portraits stared down at us from the walls of halls and classrooms. They were removed on the occasions when the superintendent of schools came to visit with guests. The teachers in my school also got together and sponsored oratorical contests and talent shows. They were not paid to do this. They devoted additional time because, for them, teaching was not just a job.

Although I do not see myself as an apologist for segregation, I cannot help feeling that I actually benefited from a school environment in which both my intellectual and human development was so genuinely cared about. In 1979 I visited one of my former elementary school teachers. She had taught me in the second or third grade and had just recently retired. She had a collection of scrapbooks full of pictures of her students over the years, and in one of them—one of the *earlier* ones—there was a picture of me. Hers was a loving, and complete, record of her years in the teaching profession. I don't think most teachers nowadays do that.

It was the role models provided by these teachers that I feel encouraged me to become a teacher. It was the preparation by my parents that allowed me to aspire to teaching, and writing, in the larger world outside Demopolis. Once I left Alabama, an entirely different set of elements began to affect my personal "ecology," but the foundation of my Alabama upbringing prepared me to meet them.

Following my own early role models, I have tried to instill in my students and in the readers of my books a sense of the larger world. Many of my early books addressed political and sociological issues—for example: *Resistance: Profiles in Nonviolence, Revolutionaries:*

Agents of Change, The War and the Protest: Vietnam, and *Profiles in Black Power.* In them, I endeavored to provide information on a level that adolescents could understand. More recently, I have written books about the Vietnamese boat people and the Cuban refugees, because the presence of these most recent immigrants to the United States is certainly a major issue in today's society and one that will affect a large percentage of our young people in one way or another. Remembering the efforts of my teachers to provide historical role models for me, I have also concentrated on writing biographies of successful blacks who have earned a place in history. My hope is that young people, black and white, will be inspired and encouraged by their example.

I cannot presume to know how well I have succeeded, or will succeed. (Another thing I learned, growing up in Alabama, is that there are no guarantees—about anything.) But my Alabama upbringing gave me the confidence to spread my own sense of humanity. And to believe in it.

A Special Heritage:

The Demopolis

Jewish Community

JACOB KOCH

Abstract definitions of the humanities abound, but Alan Koch offered one that is particular and personal: "The humanities means doing what your father tells you." Fortunately, the younger Koch had the proper example. Before Alan Koch read his father's paper to a Demopolis audience in February 1983, he declared that the "City of the People" contains several heritages. Alan Koch's modest disclaimer, however, is not meant to obscure the distinctiveness of the Demopolis Jewish community nor its contribution to Alabama and American life. Its most conspicuous literary legacy is Lillian Hellman, whose mother came from Demopolis. However, as Jacob Koch's roll-call of two centuries will show, others less well known have kept alive a tradition of success and service. Jacob Koch himself represents the spirit of cooperation which made the Jewish community a force for good in the town. For twenty-five years he managed a Rotary Club fund that makes one-percent loans to "good students of good character" who need money for college. During his tenure, this scholarship helped over thirty Marengo Countians to become doctors, lawyers, engineers, teachers, nurses, and business men and women. His excellent service is not mentioned in the essay, of course, but the history he presents indicates precision and compassion. Moving toward its elegiac conclusion, Jacob Koch's story of the Jews in Marengo County carries as much impact in print as it did in his son's presentation.

WHEN I WAS ASKED to talk about the Jewish people of Demopolis, I thought that my seventy-three years of residence here should furnish me with all the material that I needed. I was mistaken. The more I thought about it, the more I realized how little I actually knew. So at the beginning, I hereby acknowledge a great debt to Dr. Winston Smith, the late James Armistead, his lovely widow, Emogene, Mrs. Hugh Wilburn, and others for the information and assistance they have given me.

It was a surprise to me to learn that in all probability the first Jewish person to come to Demopolis to live was Mr. Isaac Marx in or about 1840. He came from Germany to Mobile when he was fifteen or sixteen years old, with nothing but a desire to work and make a living. It is believed that he worked on a river boat to pay for his transportation part of the way to Demopolis. It seems that he walked the rest of the way, selling his wares from the pack on his back. I do not know why he stopped in Demopolis and made it his home. He must have recognized the opportunities for merchandising in a settlement of planters. Suffice it to say he did stay in Demopolis and that his staying is the beginning of the Jewish contribution to our city.

It is almost impossible for us, today, to believe that a man walking down dirt roads, stopping at each home along the way and selling items that he carried on his back, could make a living, save money, establish a home and business, and make a financial success. But Isaac Marx did just that.

Mrs. Hugh Wilburn enjoys telling of his visits to her family home. Often it was late in the afternoon when he would appear, walking up the dusty Jefferson Road. Her mother and grandmother told her that they always provided him with supper, lodging, and breakfast. Afterwards he would open his pack and give them their choice of anything he had, to pay them for their kindness and hospitality. Then he would sell them whatever they needed. Mrs. Wilburn says she still has the linen tablecloth with the flag of the United States woven into the center that he gave them on one of his visits. And she also says that she wishes someone would call on her again today, at her home, with needles, pins, linens, kitchen utensils, and the like to save her a trip into town. Mrs. Wilburn remembers when, as a little girl, her mother took her to Mr. Marx's store where she bought checked gingham dress cloth for ten cents per yard.

In the ten years following his arrival in Demopolis, Isaac Marx worked, saved, and accumulated enough to have a small frame store building on the property where Mr. and Mrs. George Williams now live. It was in the early 1850s that he married and had a home near the store. Mr. and Mrs. Isaac Marx had ten children. Two died in their early childhood; the girls married and moved away. Four sons—Jacob, Edward, Julius, and Henry—stayed in Demopolis for many years and established outstanding successes in the banking and business communities of our city. The three older brothers organized and operated Marx Banking Company on the southeast corner of Washington and Walnut streets. Among their most valued employees were John Norwood and R. B. McCants. In 1912 the Robertson Banking Company bought Marx Banking Company, including the building, and made it its home until the company moved into its present location in 1975. After the sale, Jacob and Edward Marx moved to New York City where they were again most successful in the banking business. Julius Marx and his family retired to Denver, Colorado.

When Henry Marx, the youngest of the four brothers, was ready to enter the business world, his brother, Edward, joined him in establishing a horse, mule, wagon, and carriage business. They, too, were hard workers and good businessmen. Within a few years they were one of the largest stable operators in west Alabama. They introduced the famous "Studebaker" wagon to this area and flooded the countryside with them. After Henry Marx was safely on his way in the horse and mule business, Edward rejoined his brother in New York City. Henry Marx continued his business here in Demopolis until his death in 1960—during the last few years with the help of H. D. Moorer.

Mrs. Wilburn tells me that few people ever knew of his generosity when farmers needed a mule, or mules, on credit, or a loan to make a crop. I am sure that all of you know that he and his wife left their very lovely home and other property to a young lady they considered their "foster" daughter.

A final statement about Isaac Marx. Despite the problems of starting a new life at an early age in a foreign country as a peddler, making a living, and supporting a very large family, he found the time to serve his country—the Confederacy—during the Civil War.

It is my honest opinion that no history of Demopolis, and no report of its business and financial growth, could be recounted without telling of the life and contribution—the Jewish contribution—of Morris Mayer. He was truly a "merchant prince" if there ever was one.

Mayer was born in Germany in 1849. His family and the Marx family must have been friends in Germany, because it was at the suggestion of Isaac Marx that Mayer's family agreed to let him come to the United States. He came by boat—in the steerage—and arrived at Ellis Island in New York harbor when he was about fifteen years old. He had less than one dollar in his pockets when he got off the boat. He started his business career immediately by buying fifteen or twenty New York newspapers for one cent each and then selling them to his fellow immigrants for two cents each. With his profits he then bought more and expanded his operations. When he was allowed entry into New York City, he was a peddler on-his-way, selling housewares, cooking utensils, and anything else he could carry.

How he arrived in Demopolis, no one knows. But it is believed that he managed to buy a horse or mule somewhere along the way so as to furnish transportation and carry even more merchandise. He stopped first in Uniontown where Isaac Marx had friends and relatives, and then came on to Demopolis to work for Marx. Later he moved to Gainesville for a brief time, but soon returned to Demopolis where he remained the rest of his life. After working and saving for several years, he sent for his brother, Ludwig. In 1868 or 1869 the firm of Mayer Brothers was launched. It started in a very small frame building on north Walnut Street where Tom Breitling had his office at the time of his death—and where Fonville Taylor and Jerome Levy now have their offices. There is no doubt but that Morris Mayer was a genius insofar as merchandising and operating a business are concerned. The two brothers worked night and day. They saved their money and brought another brother and sister from Germany. During the next thirty years the business grew to such an extent that the Morris Mayer home was moved to the corner of Capitol and Walnut streets, and a large three-story building was erected where the house once stood—where the Robertson Banking Company is now located.

Mayer Brothers had now become a very large wholesale, jobbing, and retail business. They also owned and occupied the adjoining buildings where Culpepper Electric and Spight's Men's Store now operate. They were a large employer, with some working in the various store departments and some employed as "drummers," or traveling salesmen, who covered a radius of fifty miles around Demopolis, traveling by horse and buggy, or by boat on the river. Among them was Lee Metzger of Mobile, who later married Fannie Mayer. The names of those who passed away before 1900 are but a memory. But in my lifetime I knew and still remember a large number who were employed there and later left to establish their own businesses, homes, and families. They include the three Bley brothers, T. C. Compton, Ben Levy, Roulhac Gewin, Sam Neilson, Ben Gregory, Mr. and Mrs. Carl Michael, George Darms, my brother Isadore Koch, Bates Bell, and Sam Breitling. I also remember Mr. and Mrs. C. H. Wilson, Miss Dellie Breitling, Miss Delores Rudisill, Misses Emma and Zena Stephens, Mrs. Gertrude Mitchell, Mrs. Viola Compton Jefferson, and Sol Elkan, of course, uncle of the Bley brothers. I also knew Mrs. Floy Matthews, Dr. and Mrs. T. C. Reid, and Mrs. Cecile Hickman. You can readily see that "Mayer Brothers" not only gave employment, paid salaries, and furnished the livelihood for a large number of people, but they brought thousands of customers to Demopolis. It was by far the most successful business operation in west Alabama. I have been told that they did a million dollars a year in sales in the 1890s—an immense sum for that time. With it all, Mayer found time to serve on our city council and was a very influential director of the Robertson Banking Company.

When Morris Mayer was a young man, fate played him a strange trick, reminiscent of Longfellow's story of Miles Standish and John Alden. He was engaged to Miss Sophie Marx, daughter of Isaac Marx, but one day, being too busy at his store to escort her to a party, he asked his good friend Leonard Newhouse to fill in for him. Newhouse was happy to oblige. To Mayer's surprise and chagrin, they fell in love and Sophie married Leonard. One of their daughters, Julia, married Max Hellman of New Orleans. They were the parents of Lillian Hellman whose play "The Little Foxes" was based, in part, on her Marx forebears.

Mayer was more fortunate in his next, and real, love affair. He met, courted, and married a very lovely lady, Miss Janetta Threefoot of Meridian, Mississippi. They had a large family and I am sure that many of you have personal knowledge of their thoughtfulness, generosity, and love of their fellow man. A day never passed that a tray wasn't sent to a friend, neighbor, or someone in need.

I have fond memories of Mrs. Mayer, Mrs. Girlie Mayer Steinhart, Mrs. Fannie Mayer Metzger, and of course, Lehman Mayer. They were truly the epitome of a great family and their contribution cannot be measured.

It is with great pleasure that I tell you of the Long family and of their contributions and influence—the Jewish contribution—to our city. Moritz Long was born in Vienna, Austria, in 1848. An older brother, who was in business and living in Selma, sent for Long when he was a very young man. I do not know how or when they met, but Moritz Long fell in love with and married Miss Emma Sander in 1862; she was a native of Eutaw, Alabama.

Long owned and operated a general mercantile store on the northeast corner of Walnut and Washington streets here in Demopolis, where Cato's is now located. It was a frame building and the site was called "Long Corner" for years.

Mr. and Mrs. Long had six children—four girls and two boys. One son passed away when he was twenty years old, but the other,

Milton Long, was a most successful businessman and made a great contribution to our city. He was a World War I veteran. He was always very active in civic affairs and a very influential director of Robertson Banking Company and of Merchants Grocery Company. He owned five or six downtown stores and kept them in modernized condition. At the time of his death in 1956, in addition to bequeathing substantial sums to the Jewish Temple and for upkeep of the Jewish cemetery, he left $5,000 to the Robertson Banking Company, in trust, with the income to be used for providing school lunches, clothing, and medical treatment for needy white children in the first, second, and third grades of Demopolis Elementary School; $500 to U.S. Jones High School to be used for the purchase of equipment for a domestic science room; $500 to Birdeye Negro School of Greene County to be used for the purchase of equipment that was not bought by the state or by Greene County; $500 to the Marengo County Chapter of the American Red Cross; $500 to the Crippled Children's Clinic in Birmingham; $500 to the B'nai B'rith Home in Memphis, a charitable institution; and $500 to the Damon Runyon Cancer Fund. At his mother's death, another $500 was donated to the Demopolis High School home economics department for the purchase of needed equipment. It is quite a testament that one small family could be so concerned about the needs of others.

Who can forget the contributions to Demopolis of Jerome and Marie Levy? Throughout his adult life, he has been active in the business, religious, social, and service club activities of our community. He has served as rabbi for our temple for over forty years. He has served the city council and was president of that organization for two terms when the mayor had no vote. He has been president of the Alabama Society for Crippled Children and Adults for two terms. He has served as District Governor, Rotary International, for the district that comprises the southern half of Alabama. He has served for twelve years on the State of Alabama and national library boards. He and Marie have served on our local library board for many years. But, I am told that it is due to Marie, with her persistence and perseverance, that Demopolis has a fine new library building, complete with an exceptionally wide selection of books and research materials.

Please let me also remind you that another Jewish citizen of Demopolis, Fred A. Richard, Jr., a member of the Long family now living in Montgomery, recently gave $5,000 to our local library to buy encyclopedias and other reference books.

Miss Della Yaretzky was a lovely little lady who came to Demopolis in 1906-1907 from Tuscaloosa to teach algebra, geometry, Latin, and other subjects in our high school. Her starting salary was $30 a month. She taught here for thirty-seven years. Her students included children and grandchildren of her first pupils. When I was in high school in 1920-1924, she was the eighth-grade teacher and was still teaching the same subjects. Many people in our town my age and older remember her with love and affection and will always be grateful for the wonderful contribution she made in our educational circle and her influence on the lives of three generations of our citizens.

And now I ask your special indulgence. . . .

Back in the years of 1918-1928 especially, we had in our town a little lady about five-feet two-inches tall who in August 1915 had become a widow at age forty-one with six children and a mother to support. She had little means, but a big heart and strong determination to give her children the advantages that their playmates had. She did forget one thing, however. She never let them know how poor they really were. She loved people and all of the citizens of our town knew, admired, and respected her.

Caring for her family gave her an insight into the needs of others, so she gradually became the first "relief" or "welfare agency" in Demopolis. In those days we had quite a number of families living in Shortleaf who were out of work because the cotton mill was closed and a number at Spocari because the cement plant was "down." The Red Cross was their salvation. That organization—the only one of its kind in those days—was built and survived on voluntary contributions. This little lady, despite all of her own problems, assumed the job of helping these needy people. They came to her home at all hours. There were many times when her children would come home from school to find these unfortunates on the front porch, or if the weather was bad, in the living room, waiting to see the "Red Cross Lady." In almost all cases she would give them an order to Tom Graves's store or to John Spight's store for some meat, flour, lard, sugar, or other supplies. She had no key to her home, so it was not very surprising one night when a strange man walked in while the Red Cross Lady was talking to two of her youngest sons in the living room. When asked what he was doing, he replied, "I was told to come here and the Red Cross Lady would give me a room to stay in tonight." He was right, but he was also wrong. She sent him to a rooming house that accepted Red Cross transients.

This little lady knew in her heart and demonstrated in her actions what "charity" really meant. She was truly remarkable and I am very proud of my mother, Haannah Levy Koch, for her contribution to Demopolis.

Other Jewish women also had a part in the social, cultural, and civic life of Demopolis. Mrs. Jennie Morris Ely was a valued member of the Music Club, where she and Mrs. T. J. Turner delighted their audiences with piano duets. She was also a Literary Club member as were Mrs. Selma Bley, Mrs. Rosalie Marx, Mrs. Fannie Metzger, Mrs. Girlie Steinhart, Mrs. Marie Levy, Mrs. Sadie Louise Goldsmith, and Mrs. Hazel Koch. These ladies also participated in PTA and numerous charitable organizations.

Let me make a few statements of fact concerning the Jews of Demopolis. As I said, they came, young, with little formal education, no money, but a desire to work, save, establish a business, marry, have a home and family, and give their children all of the advantages they did not have. All of them were active in the local chamber of commerce and local school activities. A number of them served on the city council. Only one, Isidore Bley, was mayor. Six— H. B. Pate, Morris Mayer, Toby Ely, Morris Goldman, H. A. Fiebelman, and Milton Long—served on the board of directors of the Robertson Banking Company.

Isaac Marx served in the Civil War. Dr. Henry Bley, Milton Long, and Adrian Pizer, uncle of Melvin Levy, served in the First World War. Mr. Pizer gave his life.

Florian Koch, Melvin Levy, Fred Richard, Ed Levy, Jr., and I served in World War II. My son, Jack Koch, served in the Korean conflict. During World War I, Sadie Louise Morris Goldsmith, daughter of Mr. and Mrs. Leon Morris, sold more Liberty Bonds than anyone else in this area and was recognized for her service to her country in many newspaper accounts.

Many Jewish citizens were notable in various categories. B. J. Levy was a member of the school board when the old school was built on the corner between Walnut and Main streets. He and fellow board members, Dr. Cocke and William Herbert, said that the building was large enough to accommodate the town's students for all future time. In later years, school board members included Isidore Koch, Edward Levy, Melvin "Stick" Levy, and Florian Koch.

I think specific mention should here be made of Dr. Jerre Levy who does research at the University of Chicago and is known nationally for her work in biology.

We have had our cemetery since 5 November 1878. It was a gift to the Jewish people of Demopolis from Mr. and Mrs. John C. Webb, Sr. In 1890, a lot on the corner of Main and Monroe streets was purchased from Mr. and Mrs. J. T. Jones, and a large white temple was erected. It included Sunday school rooms and a balcony for the choir. The choir consisted of Mrs. Pearl Bailey, Mr. and Mrs. Stanhope Brasfield, Mrs. Fannie Mayer Metzger, Mrs. Girlie Mayer Steinhart, Captain T. C. Reid, and Lehman Mayer. My father, Henry Koch, also sang in the choir, as well as in all of the other church choirs in Demopolis. Our original organ was an old-fashioned type which had to be pumped by hand, and I, among others, was a "pumper." Mrs. Jennie Ely, a skilled musician and music teacher in the public schools, was the first organist. She was later succeeded by Mrs. Vera Howze at the keyboard. Before 10 April 1890, the date of the dedication of the temple, services were held in private homes and later above a downtown store.

After the membership of the congregation dwindled, the temple, which was beginning to show signs of age, became too large and a smaller, more compact building was constructed inside the larger one. When it was completed, the outer building was carefully demolished. Thus the old gave birth to the new, which is still in use.

During my boyhood there were at least twenty Jewish-operated business firms in Demopolis. When they closed for our High Holy Days, Demopolis looked like a ghost town. Today there are only two—Jerome Levy Travel Agency and Rosenbush Furniture, owned by Bert Rosenbush, Jr., grandson of its founder, Julius Rosenbush; it is the oldest family-operated firm in the city.

I have checked with the City of Demopolis Police Department and the Sheriff of Marengo County. There is no record that we could find where a Jew has been incarcerated in our jails.

Demopolis is blessed in that all of our people, regardless of race or creed, are as one. The Baraca Sunday School Class of the First Baptist Church selected Jerome Levy as the Demopolis Man of the Year in 1947. Also, when our neighbors across the street from the temple were in the process of building their parish house, the Episcopal Sunday school classes were held in the Jewish temple.

In my lifetime I have known about 160 Jewish people in Demopolis. Now time has taken its toll. Today we have ten Jews in our town population of about 7,500 and nine of these ten are in their seventies. The tenth is over fifty. In Marengo County with a population of about 25,000, we have thirteen Jews—the ten in Demopolis and three in the Nathan Levy family in Linden.

It appears that we are following the example of our illustrious founders, the royal French settlers. They came, but they did not stay. So, too, the Jews came, established homes and businesses. Now the children of those families, during the past twenty-five years, have gone to college, have become professional men and women, and have moved to larger cities where advantages for them are greater. And strange as it may seem, there is not a merchant among them.

We, who are so proud to be a part of our city's historic past and present will, sadly for us, have no part in its future. Our children, who are our greatest asset, have each in his or her own way, contributed to the cultural and religious life of their adopted cities. Incidentally, a large number, comparatively speaking, have settled in Montgomery including Helen Long Levi, Maxine Goodman Endel, Fred Richard, Babette Levy Wampold, and Jack and Alan Koch.

Surely when the history of Demopolis is written by someone more qualified than I, the record of the Jewish contribution will be a shining light to all of us—both Jews and Christians—and we will all be justly proud.

Growing Up Baptist

In Anniston, Alabama:

The Legacy of the Reverend

Charles R. Bell, Jr.

WAYNE FLYNT

James Wayne Flynt's production is enough to intimidate a beginning scholar, and his academic performance over the last twenty years is impressive, but his personal qualifications as an Alabamian and a historian are what make this essay a model of its form. It joins his feeling for his own family's history with his skills as a researcher and a writer to show what impact one person can have on a church, a community, and a growing boy. Though it is more directly personal, the essay is characteristic of Flynt's other writings. The stories he heard about poor whites in northeast Alabama, whose suffering reached Old Testament proportions, gave rise to his best-known book, *Dixie's Forgotten People*. His other scholarship—four books and about thirty essays—is also suffused with the same sense of particular people and particular places. Through careful research and analysis he has unveiled new insights into the people who often held fast to their faith, to their arts and crafts, and to their hope for a better political future. Some of these Southerners became embodiments of the dream of democracy. Given an opportunity, they improved their lives and shared their prosperity with others. Flynt has explored topics ranging from religious and denominational history to those relating to labor, education, and politics. He is now completing a study of the tenant farmer system in the South.

PARKER MEMORIAL BAPTIST CHURCH does not even look like a Baptist church. There are no Corinthian columns, red bricks, or broad porticoes. Dominating the important corner of 12th and Quintard in Anniston, Alabama, it rises in majestic glory, a Victorian tribute to God's presence in a small Southern industrial town. It was constructed in 1890-1891 of sandstone, now darkened by age, and is dominated by its bell tower, presently to become a roost for pigeons and a peril to worshipers.

Even the church's name seemed unbaptistic. Who ever heard of a Baptist church named in memory of a person? Calvary Baptist or Shiloh, or even some harmless numerical designation like First or Second Baptist seemed entirely biblical (after all, there is a 1st and 2nd Samuel, 1st and 2nd Chronicles, and even 1st, 2nd, and 3rd John); but churches named for people seemed vaguely idolatrous or perhaps even papist.

When my family moved to Anniston in 1956, leaving an exuberant young congregation in Dothan, I was not about to exchange Calvary Baptist for Parker Memorial, the austere concrete block church with folding chairs for the somber beauty and padded pews of Parker's sanctuary. Calvary seemed the proper incubator for Baptist ministerial students; Parker the kind of place where they perished.

My parents, who received all these impressions with mature patience and some trepidation over what kind of religious home I might select for us, were therefore shocked when I announced after attending one service of a youth revival that I had moved my letter to Parker Memorial. They joined me the following Sunday and we settled into a pattern of religious life common to many Baptist congregations: Sunday school and Training Union, Wednesday night suppers served by a friendly black woman who could cook our food, attend our weddings and funerals, but not our preaching services. There were summer youth retreats in Panama City, fellowships following Anniston High School football games, rigorous choir practices under the intimidating but immensely competent choir leader/organist Griff Perry (who amazed us all by his capacity to drive the organ to thunderous crescendoes). Bible sword drills, young people's speaker's tournaments, Vacation Bible School, and county-wide Associational Youth rallies made sure young people avoided most of the sins of dance and drink about which we were constantly warned. They needn't have worried; there was little time left for iniquities of the flesh. Both casual friendships and serious dating naturally turned inward upon those we knew so well.

Because the congregation was affluent, at least by Anniston standards, it dominated much of the social and economic life of the city. Its rivals—the spectacular Church of St. Michael and All Angels, Grace Episcopal, or First Methodist—lacked either its size and scope of programs, or its historic building and energy. From the ranks of its youth came a regular procession of appointees to the Naval Academy or students who distinguished themselves at fine colleges. Among its influential members was Harry M. Ayers, publisher of the *Anniston Star*. Ayers was an uncharacteristically liberal man for a small Southern town, who had been offered the ambassadorship to Sweden by Harry S. Truman and who endorsed a Roman Catholic for the presidency in 1960. And there was Charles R. Bell, president of Anniston National Bank.

"Captain" Bell crossed my life more than once. A kindly, even godly man if bankers are allowed such exalted designations, he directed the bank that owned the land at Shady Glen where my grandfather was a sharecropper during the 1920s and 1930s. My grandfather had often praised "Captain" Bell as the best and fairest of landlords, a man who had tried, to no avail, to persuade him to purchase the farm during the 1930s using as payment his share of the cotton crop. It was a measure of Bell's respect in the church and community that his son was called as pastor of Parker Memorial in the 1930s and that he lasted as long as he did. But that is getting ahead of the story.

Parker only barely became a church at all. The first Baptist church in the new industrial town of Anniston was as carefully planned as was the rest of the city. To the Tyler and Noble families that established the community, churches contributed stability, decorum, and a spiritual dimension to life. When some members of First Baptist decided to build a second Baptist church across town at Twelfth Street in 1887, the pastor of the older congregation so resented the missionary effort that he refused to deliver the invocation at the organization of the new church or preach from its pulpit. Despite his recalcitrance, Twelfth Street enrolled as charter members many of the city's most prominent people, including Dr. and Mrs. T. W. Ayers.

A native of Georgia, Ayers purchased his first newspaper there at the age of eighteen. Later he established a paper in Jacksonville, Alabama, and then opened a drugstore in Anniston sometime during 1883. Using the earnings from his drugstore, he attended medical school in Baltimore, returning to Anniston in 1886 to practice medicine. He founded and edited the *Alabama Medical Journal*, edited Anniston's daily, *The Hot Blast*, established the local chamber of commerce, and became the first president of Alabama's Good Roads Association. Always interested in politics, he was also chairman of the fourth district Democratic Congressional Campaign Committee for six critical years during the Populist uprising of the 1890s.

He devoted the same energy to the new Baptist congregation that he lavished on secular affairs, serving as deacon, superintendent of the Sunday school, chairman of the building committee, and organizer and president of the first Baptist Young People's Union. A man who combined so many skills with such obvious spiritual devotion surprised few with his announcement in 1900 that he intended to embark on yet another career, that of Baptist missionary. According to Ayers's account, while on his knees praying one day, "there came as clear as if there had been an audible voice the command to go as a missionary doctor to China and I immediately wrote . . . offering my services as a foreign missionary."[1]

---

[1] *The Anniston Star* (5 January 1954).

In 1901, Dr. Ayers, his wife, and three of their children booked passage for China. Applying his indefatigable energies to Shantung Province, he built two hospitals and was twice decorated by the president of the Republic of China for work during plague and civil war. After he returned from China in 1926 because of his wife's failing health, the Chinese government constructed a monument in his honor. Ayers's grandson returned to China after the Second World War with a United Nations team and found the monument still standing amidst the rubble of Baptist schools, church, and hospital. Japanese and Communist troops had left the statue, perhaps impressed with its simple inscription: "He treated the rich and poor alike."

In a sense, that classless inscription inspired a generation of urban middle class church people devoted to moral uplift, and it also animated the Baptist congregation. Established during an era of shifting religious values, the church exhibited many aspects of new religious thought. The first pastor, Dr. G. A. Nunnally, was deeply committed to education and left the church in 1889 after a two-year pastorate to become president of Mercer University in Georgia.

The new pastor was chosen not in the conventional Baptist way, but by Duncan T. Parker who was not even a member of the congregation. Parker was president of the First National Bank of Anniston and husband of the church's first organist. He informed the pulpit committee that he would contribute $1,000 a year toward the pastor's salary if it would call Dr. George B. Eager from his pastorate in Danville, Virginia. Such an offer was too good to turn down, and the handsome, scholarly Eager preached his first sermon on 20 October 1889. His involvement in public issues was as intense as that of his parishioner, Dr. Ayers. In later years, as pastor of First Baptist Church in Montgomery, Eager championed women's rights and other political and economic reforms. But Eager's courageous stand for moral principles at Parker led to his resignation in 1892. The occasion was a controversy with the Calhoun Club, a social organization to which several prominent Parker members belonged. The club served liquor and Eager scolded the members in a sermon so strong that the club threatened legal action. Club members retaliated in the press and demanded that he retract his charges. This he steadfastly refused to do. Although a majority of his congregation supported him, the division within his church convinced him that only his resignation could heal the wounds.

During Eager's pastorate, Duncan Parker lost both his eldest son and wife, and in memorial to them he offered to build the young church an imposing edifice. Although Duncan Parker died before the building was completed in 1891, his $85,000 constructed a worthy memorial, complete with magnificent stained glass windows, each memorializing a member of the Parker family. The name was changed from the pedestrian Twelfth Street to the imposing Parker Memorial (locals soon dropped the "Memorial" and "Baptist" as useless information; everyone knew what was meant by Parker Church).

Subsequent pastors maintained both the social involvement and the penchant for controversy that were characteristic of Eager's tenure. Dr. Samuel Clopton of Richmond, Virginia, replaced Eager but he had a short and stormy pastorate as well. He was married to a much younger, independent-minded woman who refused to hold church dinners in her home. Further, when the Ladies' Aid Society, which traditionally raised money to pay church debts by sponsoring a theatrical event, agreed to the suggestion of the wife of a wealthy deacon and Sunday school superintendent of performing a blackface minstrel show in the church auditorium, Clopton was appalled at such sacrilege. The woman's husband resigned as deacon and Clopton resigned as pastor.

Joshua Hill Foster, formerly pastor of Birmingham's Ruhama Baptist Church, served a long pastorate from 1896 until 1909. Like his predecessors, he was a well-educated man from a prominent family, one that had furnished a president to the University of Alabama. He would himself serve as a college president after his tenure in Anniston. Foster brought a sensitive social consciousness to the industrial town. During a lengthy strike in Birmingham, he brooded about strikers who were literally starving. When his cow disappeared he searched for it until told that some miners had been seen butchering the animal. Foster shrugged: "Well, they were starving. They're welcome to the cow."[2] Traditional in many ways

---

[2]Joshua Hill Foster, *Sixty-Four Years a Minister* (Wilmington NC, 1948) 54.

(he persuaded Parker to avoid fund-raising festivals and continued the strong prohibitionist sentiment of the church's pastors), he began a mission at a local cotton mill to minister to poorer whites, and he also brought the Chautauqua to Anniston.

William F. Yarborough, a Mississippi native, succeeded Foster. The new pastor's social conscience matched Foster's. Parker was Alabama's sixth largest Baptist church in membership and third in contributions. But because it chiefly represented the privileged, Yarborough advocated the "abolition of class spirit in the church life, insisting that there was no distinction" between men in the sight of God. Animated by that theology, he persuaded the church to employ a social worker whose ministry was directed toward the city's mill families. Miss Linda Martin of Springfield, Missouri, a trained social worker, conducted Sunday school on the sabbath, but used Parker's building in the mill district for social ministries during the week.[3] Yarborough left Parker in 1916 to become executive secretary of the Alabama Baptist Executive Board, the highest office in the state Baptist hierarchy.

Dr. Leon Latimer from Sylacauga pastored Parker from 1916 until 1921. He was a strong advocate of the YMCA and of extending ministries to the thousands of soldiers being trained at the newly created Camp McClellan just north of town. When Latimer left to become pastor in Greenville, South Carolina, Parker Memorial called Dr. J. T. McGlothlin, a robust, aggressive pastor from Franklin, Kentucky, whose brother was the president of Furman University. McGlothlin continued both the church's rapid membership growth and its tradition of strong-minded and controversial pastors. In 1928 he divided the community by openly supporting Republican Herbert Hoover for president in opposition to the anti-prohibitionist Catholic Alfred E. Smith. When he left in 1932 to become business manager of the Southern Baptist Sunday School

---

[3]"Parker Memorial Baptist Church, Anniston, Alabama, 1887-1937," anonymous manuscript, Church Records Division, Alabama Baptist Historical Society (ABHS), Samford University Library, Birmingham AL. Hereafter Bell Papers.

Board, Parker Memorial summoned one of its own as pastor, Charles R. Bell, Jr.[4]

In my teenage years I noticed the downcast eyes and quick digressions when Charlie Bell's name was mentioned, which it seldom was despite his long tenure. The sense of unease fascinated and perplexed me. So it was with considerable interest that I anticipated his return during a church anniversary in the late 1950s. Although several former pastors were still alive, Bell was asked to preach. His sermon gave no clue to the disquietude of so many members; it was well-conceived and brilliantly delivered. Even from the distance of twenty-five years I remember that it concerned umbrellas and how the church should both shield people and radiate God's presence into the world. For me to remember a sermon for a quarter of a century, it had to be good. When a love affair with history interrupted my ministerial career, I finally got my chance to unravel the mysterious relationship between the Rev. Charles R. Bell, Jr., and Parker Memorial Church.

Charlie Bell grew up in the affluence of a small-town banking family, wealthy compared to Anniston's pipe shop and textile mill workers or rural Calhoun County sharecroppers. Anniston was a town whose classes were separated both by race and by neighborhood. West of the main shopping district of Noble Street were the pipe shops, railroad yards, and textile mills with their adjacent neighborhoods of workers. They formed their own subcommunities, such as Glen Addie and Blue Mountain, complete with local grocery stores, playgrounds, and most certainly churches. Here and there black enclaves sprang up, even crossing Quintard in south Anniston to intrude on the perimeter of the Anniston Country Club. When we first lived in Anniston in the late 1940s, only a high fence and an alley separated our house from a black neighborhood. We lived in East Anniston and that was important. Living in East Anniston determined where you attended church, which group you ran with at Anniston High School, and gave your gen-

---

[4]Harry M. Ayers, *Parker Memorial Baptist Church, Anniston, Alabama, 1887-1937* (n.p., n.p.) 31.

eral standing in the community. True, there were areas where the two Annistons met—on high school athletic teams, at Baptist Associational youth rallies, and especially dating—but all such occasions provided parents with opportunities for lectures on marrying people of similar backgrounds or how "old so-and-so" was really very nice but somehow not our kind of person. On Saturdays yet another stratum was added to the town's population as hundreds of country people descended on the stores. Old men whittled in front of the courthouse, and if you were not careful you discovered why signs dotted Noble Street forbidding spitting on the sidewalks.

Young Charlie Bell's house, not far from Parker, was accommodating though not ostentatious. In fact that held true for the entire Bell family. They were well-to-do committed Baptists without being stuffy or calling attention to themselves. Parker was filled with that kind of Baptist. Set on a ministerial course by his devout family, a warm creative congregation, and a Baptist church that was unusually open and ecumenical, Bell enrolled at the denomination's Howard College. But he chafed under the constraints and parochialism of the place. He was a free-spirited young man with a residue of the world about him; he attended football games without paying and was not overly pious by Howard's standards.

After several years he transferred to a more challenging Baptist institution, Brown University in Rhode Island, which had lost its denominational distinctiveness while gaining a splendid faculty and a reputation for fine scholarship. From the scintillating world of Brown he pursued a safer course into the Baptist pulpit by taking his degree from Southern Baptist Theological Seminary in Louisville, Kentucky. There he came under the spell of W. O. Carver, beloved professor of Comparative Religion and Missions, and H. W. Tribble who taught theology. Brown and Southern left their mark on him: "I had a whole new vista of life to open that I had just never known was there. It intrigued me, and it fascinated me; I began reading and I began reaching out for every possible source of information that I could get hold of."[5]

---

[5]Oral history with Charles R. Bell, Jr., 28 January 1972.

Charles Bell returned in 1932 to the congregation where he was raised. It was a moment of rejoicing for the Bell and Ayers families in a world fast coming apart. The depression had hit Anniston hard, closing many of its shops and mills and bringing labor strife to those remaining open. In the rural districts of Calhoun County, where my grandfather sharecropped on "Captain Bell's place," poverty reigned. That perplexing world soon caught the attention of Parker's new preacher.

Actually the Reverend Mr. Bell was rather traditional in many ways. He struggled over the ethics of performing marriages for the divorced, protested the use of rationed sugar for the production of liquor, and persuaded his church to sponsor its own missionary to Nigeria.[6] The generosity of the church toward unfortunates was broadened by Bell's international vision, but even that found precedent in Dr. T. W. Ayers's long sojourn in China and in the vigorous internationalism of his son, Harry, who made the *Anniston Star* one of the handful of consistently liberal newspapers in Alabama. Harry Ayers relished young Bell's vision and together they stimulated Parker Memorial to new heights. From his position of power as teacher of the quasi-independent Baraca Sunday School Class, Harry Ayers helped establish the International House at nearby Jacksonville State University for the exchange of international students and provided financial support for missionary Christie Poole.[7] The church sent money to India in 1937, to Lebanon for the purchase of free medicines for poverty-stricken patients of American University's hospital in 1938, and to China for war relief in 1941.[8]

But as Bell confessed, education had stretched his mind and opened new vistas. Perhaps because he was a bachelor until the

---

[6]W. O. Carver to Charles R. Bell, Jr., 18 January 1941; Sam Hobbs to Bell, Jr., 14 May 1942; John H. Bankhead to Bell, Jr., 27 April 1942, Bell Papers.

[7]Erman L. Crew, *History of the Baraca Class, Parker Memorial Baptist Church, Anniston, Alabama, 1904-1976* (n.p., n.p.). Copy in ABHS.

[8]H. M. Cox to Bell, Jr., 20 July 1937; Khalil Watim to Bell, Jr., 23 April 1938; Henry R. Luce to Bell, Jr., 28 November 1941, Bell Papers.

late 1930s when he married Ann Cole, a wealthy young woman, he struggled particularly hard to deepen the quality of relationships within his congregation. The method he chose for this ministry of deepened spirituality was a strange one which had first attracted him at Brown. The Oxford Group, or Buchmanite Movement, had been founded in England by Frank Buchman. Devoted to pure, simplified Christianity, it encouraged mutual confession and restitution. What often followed was release from guilt and an overwhelming sense of gratitude and happiness. As Bell described it, the Oxford Group "brought the most powerful influence into my life . . . for righteousness and goodness. It helped me to see myself as I had never seen myself before."

In addition to being a young, idealistic, and naive minister, Bell was a compelling pulpit orator, and members of his congregation were attracted by his obvious dedication to a more serious discipleship. Soon about fifty people, most of them young, were meeting regularly. They confessed sins, made restitution, shared testimonies, and developed a close fellowship. Bell had intended to expand the Oxford Group into a new kind of church fellowship, but the religious intimacy and self-revelation demanded by the group repelled many members and excited the jealousy of others. To Bell, the Oxford Group was a saving remnant that took the ethical and spiritual demands of the Bible seriously and could radiate this new discipleship throughout the church. To many members, it was Charlie's clique, a self-righteous, exclusive group that laid claim to a special holiness.

In the early days of his ministry, Bell's obvious sincerity provoked disbelief and comical dilemmas. He insisted on paying for football games he had attended without tickets while a student at Howard College. When officials praised his honesty and told him to forget it, he persisted until they accepted his checks. He insisted on paying more for his cabin on an around-the-world cruise because he was charged too little in a misunderstanding. He refused to sign the standard oath of allegiance to defend the United States when applying for a passport, creating a bureaucratic deadlock that finally forced the State Department to offer him not one but two alternative Christian oaths.[9] Bell himself conceded years later that his youthful immaturity and idealism caused much of the trouble at Parker. Some elements of the Oxford Group were faddish and he did not attempt to form such groups in subsequent parishes.[10]

But Charlie Bell brought a far deeper and more threatening vision of the gospel to Parker than the Oxford Group. The Buchmanite controversy might evoke vigorous debate within the church and frivolous gossip around town, but Bell's devotion to rural cooperatives, socialism, justice for workers and blacks, and a host of other liberal causes, seemed to threaten the entire underpinnings of Southern society.

In 1936, while still a bachelor and after four years as pastor in Anniston, Bell requested a six-months leave of absence to travel and study. The trip was a turning point in his life. He traveled to Europe with a group, but then they parted ways. Bell sailed through the Suez to India where he talked with Mohandas Gandhi in his home and observed the wretched poverty of Indians under British colonial rule. He then traveled to Singapore, China, and to Japan where he stayed with a Mr. Hourinuchi, whom he had come to know through the Oxford Movement. Both he and his wife were enthusiastic Christians, and they remained close friends until Hourinuchi became Japanese ambassador to the United States and relations between the two countries worsened.

While in Japan, Bell met Toyohiko Kagawa, a celebrated Christian leader who had begun urban social ministries and cooperatives in Tokyo. Bell attended his revivals and an intensive training session for his followers and associates. He spent time in his home and was obviously thoroughly converted to cooperative principles. Kagawa toured the U.S. in 1936 to mixed reactions, and Charles persuaded his younger brother, Tartt, then an impressionable student at Tulane University, to attend Kagawa's lectures in New Orleans; the Bell family had another convert to cooperatives.

---

[9]Oscar Causey to Bell, Jr., 15 May 1936; D. M. Key to Bell, Jr., 14 May 1936; R. B. Shipley, Chief, Passport Division, to Bell, Jr., 17 April 1936, Bell Papers.

[10]Oral history with Charles R. Bell, Jr.

During Kagawa's tour, a Baptist missionary friend in Japan, who also was a Kagawa disciple, sent Bell a copy of a letter from the editor of the Texas *Baptist Standard*. The editor relayed the enormous interest in Kagawa's visit to Dallas, where the First Baptist Church could not accommodate all the requests for seats. But he inquired privately about rumors circulating through the South that the eminent Japanese Christian was also a socialist.[11] The letter must have amused Bell, who voted three times for Socialist party presidential candidate Norman Thomas. Although Bell did not flaunt his socialism from the pulpit, he did make it clear that the existing distribution of goods in the 1930s was not consistent with Christian ethics.

When Bell came to Anniston, he vowed he could not share conditions there unless he "moved across the railroad tracks," a goal he never achieved.[12] But as the depression settled over the community, not even the tracks shielded his view. When President Roosevelt wrote clergymen in 1935 seeking reports on conditions in their communities, Bell minced no words. Conditions were wretched, especially housing for low-income blacks and whites: "Living in the most degrading circumstances, hounded by loan sharks and getting nothing for a crop is a fair description of the life so many of our people know. Our government should do something about it."[13]

But he was unwilling to wait for federal programs. When he returned from Japan, he launched a rigorous study of the cooperative movement. He wrote friends at Brown University for information as well as the Cooperative League of the United States. He gathered information about cooperative farms in Raleigh, North Carolina, Jacksonville, Florida, and elsewhere. In July 1937 he visited the Delta Cooperative Farm in Hillhouse, Mississippi. He also studied

---

[11]Tartt Bell to Bell, Jr., undated, but some time in March 1936; F. M. McConnell to Rev. Herman S. Ray, 19 February 1936, Bell Papers.

[12]K. Brooke Anderson to Bell, Jr., 5 May 1937, Bell Papers.

[13]Bell, Jr., to Franklin D. Roosevelt, 3 October 1935, PPF 21-A, Clergy Letters, Alabama, Box 4, FDR Library, Hyde Park, New York.

carefully Jim Perry's Sky Valley Farm at Zirconia, North Carolina, and another in Copiah County, Mississippi. Patterned after Kagawa's socialist spiritual community, the farms were designed as self-supporting economic units. He also developed a lifelong friendship with Clarence Jordan, a seminary classmate who founded Koinonia Farm in Georgia.[14]

Excited by what he saw and heard, he determined to establish his own cooperative outside Anniston. He intended to move there (at last, "across the tracks") and create a cooperative farm, working it in conjunction with his church. But Parker's leaders denied their support and the project never materialized. He actually planted and harvested crops himself and conducted a camp there for the black children, but the cooperative features were never implemented. Later attempts in Madison, Wisconsin, failed also, and he gave up that dream as he did the Oxford Group. The best he could do was persuade Parker to contribute to Sky Valley Farm.[15]

Bell's deepening involvement in the rural cooperative movement branched into many subsidiary relationships. Several liberal ministerial friends gave his name to Lucy Randolph Mason, a native Virginian who came to Atlanta in 1937 to help improve the image of the C.I.O. in the South. She assisted the Textile Workers Organizing Committee which was particularly active in the Anniston area. She used Bell as one of her Alabama contacts and he sent her names of liberal ministers in the state who might be sympathetic to labor unionism. There weren't many names to send. But his respect within the community did allow him to mediate a textile strike at the Utica Mills, where he knew the manager well, and advise on a later strike at the Lengel-Fencil Mill.[16] Later, the National Religion and Labor Foundation asked him to coordinate its work in

---

[14]Anderson to Bell, Jr., 5 May 1937; E. R. Brown to Bell, Jr., 13 May 1937; Gemiann Patton to Anne and Charlie Bell, Jr., September 1943; Arle Brooks to Bell, Jr., 27 July 1943; Clarence Jordan to Bell, Jr., 13 July 1944, Bell Papers.

[15]Oral history with Charles R. Bell, Jr.; Annie G. Perry, et al. to Bell, Jr., 19 September 1943, Bell Papers.

[16]Lucy R. Mason to Bell, Jr., 25 July, 25 August, and 25 October 1937; oral history with Charles R. Bell, Jr.

Alabama, and William Mitch and other U.M.W.-C.I.O. leaders in Birmingham met with him to try to develop more community support for unions in the Anniston area.

Labor could not co-opt Bell into a narrowly partisan position. In fact he wrote U.A.W.-C.I.O. Vice President Walter Reuther that labor needed a broader vision than that of just another "narrow economic pressure group." Reuther agreed that the real hope of American labor was to advance democracy during peacetime with the same zeal with which the nation pursued victory in wartime.[17]

The preservation of caste was even more fundamental to the survival of Anniston's social mores than the maintenance of economic class boundaries. And once again Bell ran counter to the white community. From his earliest days in Anniston, he had crossed the color line. In the fall of 1932, shortly after arriving back home, he met with Dr. George Washington Carver at Tuskegee Institute. During subsequent years he attended meetings with Anniston's black leaders, ran camps for black children, corresponded with black college students, and finally, toward the end of his Anniston ministry, defied one of the most sacred racial taboos by entertaining blacks at a Christmas party in his home.

That such racial iconoclasm was genuine is clearly shown in his correspondence. Robert Lee Moffett was a young Anniston black who knew Bell's family well. When Moffett departed for college in Philadelphia, Bell kept in touch, deepening the relationship with probing questions about Moffett's studies and philosophy of life. The young black responded with frankness and candor. How could Congress speak seriously of equality for all people and reject anti-lynching and anti-poll tax bills? Did such action correspond to the notion that "all men are created equal"? Perhaps he told Bell more than the minister cared to know:

> This is what life means to me: I cannot have a job equal to that of a white man with the same preparation and qualification; I cannot enjoy the things of nature as God put them here on earth be-

---

[17]Willard Uphaus to Bell, Jr., 14 February 1939; Yelverton Cowherd to Bell, Jr., 6 December 1941; Walter P. Reuther to Bell, Jr., 8 July 1944, Bell Papers.

cause of some unscrupulous men; I am considered to be inferior to the white man because of my heritage and color; I am separated and discriminated against because I was born in an unfortunate position.

The church was far from the teachings of Christ, but Moffett harbored no hatred toward whites: "Of a truth I can say that some of my best friends are white [such] as you and many others. I write these things to you because you are broad minded and can understand my feelings."[18]

Whoever was to blame for Robert Lee Moffett's world, it certainly was not Charlie Bell. As he often did, Bell turned from the personal to the political realm for amelioration, lobbying Alabama's liberal congressional delegation for precisely the kind of changes Moffett sought. But he soon discovered that their liberalism did not extend quite so far. When he urged Senator Hugo Black, a fellow Alabama Baptist, to support the anti-lynching bill then before Congress, Black demurred: "It is a real pleasure for me to know that Parker Memorial Baptist Church has a Minister with the liberal views expressed by you in your communication. It is my earnest hope that our denomination may have more who are willing to view economic and social abuses with your own liberal vision." However, he wrote that the federal legislation would not prevent lynchings and might even encourage them.[19]

Bell next urged repeal of the poll tax which disfranchised hundreds of thousands of poor Alabama citizens of both races. Hugo Black's successor, Senator Lister Hill, was a thoroughgoing liberal on most issues, but Bell had asked too much: "I regret that I do not find myself in accord with your views with reference to Federal action on the poll tax. You and I are so much in accord on so many other matters and seem to be fundamentally so much in agreement in the cause of human rights, human progress and human welfare that I particularly regret our difference of views in the

---

[18]George W. Carver to Bell, Jr., 26 October 1932; Robert Lee Moffett to Bell, Jr., 4 June 1944, Bell Papers.

[19]Hugo L. Black to Bell, Jr., 10 May 1937, Bell Papers.

poll tax matter." Senator John H. Bankhead also opposed federal action, worrying that it would further expand federal powers at the expense of state rights.[20]

Charlie Bell was a stubborn man and he would not relent. He encouraged like-minded racial liberals across the South and began publicizing his own views.[21] His essay "Race in the Deep South" appeared in a 1944 issue of *Fellowship*, the publication of the Fellowship of Reconciliation. That same year he penned an essay entitled "A Southern Approach to the Color Issue" for *Christian Century*, suggesting prophetically that Southern blacks should adopt a strategy of peaceful noncooperation. Bell was intrigued by Gandhi's civil disobedience in India and believed it might work in American race relations.

Though he did not advertise his views in Anniston, word of his biracial activities circulated through his congregation. One anonymous member wrote him in January 1944:

> There is an ugly rumor going the rounds of town which I am sure must be untrue, namely what you did during the holidays, entertain a bunch of negroes in your home, that you and your wife sat at the table with them and entertained them in your living room. . . .
>
> I can hardly believe this rumor, but if it is true you ought to explain it to your congregation and explain why you lowered yourself lower than a negro.

If true, Bell should resign. In an ironic but revealing climax, the outraged parishioner concluded:

> If you had gone down the streets of Anniston blind drunk, the people of Anniston might forgive that, but they will never forgive nor forget this evidence on your part that you feel that a negro is the equal of a white person.[22]

---

[20]Lister Hill to Bell, Jr., 2 November 1942; J. H. Bankhead to Bell, Jr., 28 October 1942, Bell Papers.

[21]Virginius Dabney to Bell, Jr., 22 March 1944, Bell Papers.

[22]"A Member" to Bell, Jr., 31 January 1944, Bell Papers.

At least Bell got the outraged critic to church; he promised to attend Sunday to hear Bell defend himself.

That letter was subtle compared to another that featured four newspaper articles reporting black rapes and murders of whites. The gruesome montage had a cryptic message attached:

> Since the negro is the object of your particular fanaticism I am enclosing clippings which are evidences of their gentle, Christlike, un-brutal characters.
>
> The next time you throw a nigger party you ought to give the item to the social editor of the paper. There are a few people in town who have not heard of your former party in your home.
>
> Many of the people who go to hear you do so from curiosity and not to hear the word of God.[23]

Bell tendered his resignation within months of these messages, but in retrospect he believed his racial views played little role in the final denouement. Few Parker members shared his racial liberalism, but they were more tolerant of his eccentricities on the issue than were his anonymous critics.[24]

Perhaps his solace did not come from white liberals at all. During a 1939 resignation crisis, Bell received a letter from an Anniston black woman, Louise J. Moses. She had heard that he planned to leave Anniston and could not let him depart without letting him know how far-reaching had been his influence:

> We, who represent the minor group of the population have appreciated every brave word spoken for us through Christ. A gradual change is taking place in the hearts of those you have touched. You have been a great inspiration to many of us directly and indirectly. The days of indecision, perhaps, to follow shall call for strength, but remember—the message you have been called to bear cannot die; for "the seed has been sown" and "the bread cast out upon the waters."[25]

------

[23]Anonymous to Bell, Jr., undated but January 1944, Bell Papers.

[24]Oral history with Charles R. Bell, Jr.

[25]Louise J. Moses to Bell, Jr., 13 October 1939, Bell Papers.

It was his interest in racial justice and dignity for the poor that involved him in the Southern Conference for Human Welfare. Charles Dobbins, his Howard College classmate, had settled in Anniston during the 1930s where for some years he published the *Anniston Times*. Bell wrote a column for the *Times* each week. He and Dobbins attended the organizational meeting of the Southern Conference in Birmingham. His most vivid memories of the 1938 event were meeting Eleanor Roosevelt and Eugene "Bull" Connor's vigorous imposition of racial segregation on the delegates in the Municipal Auditorium.[26]

The American Civil Liberties Union tried to persuade Bell to become its Alabama state chairman in 1938, but Bell, deeply enmeshed in enough controversy already, declined. That did not keep him from bombarding Alabama's congressional delegation with protests against the red-baiting Dies Committee. That committee, better known in later years as the House Un-American Activities Committee, labeled as communist every liberal organization from the C.I.O. to the World Council of Churches. Congressman William Bankhead seemed little interested, but Sam Hobbs of Alabama's 4th Congressional District was inclined to terminate funding to the committee as Bell proposed.[27]

Despite his iconclasm on a multitude of domestic issues, it was his vision of a Christian's responsibility in international relations that provoked the final split in his congregation. Bell was exceptionally well informed on international issues and, as usual, had strong opinions regarding proper moral conduct. Like many 1930s liberals, he vigorously opposed U.S. involvement in the European war that began in 1939. Both he and his brother, Tartt, were greatly influenced by isolationist Senator Gerald Nye whose senate committee had concluded that international bankers had manipulated America into the First World War without strategic or ethical justification. Bell believed British imperialism in India was an issue as

---

[26]Louise O. Charlton to Bell, Jr., 29 August 1938, Bell Papers; oral history with Charles R. Bell, Jr.

[27]Harry F. Ward to Bell, Jr., 15 November 1938; W. B. Bankhead to Bell, Jr., 15 December 1938; Sam Hobbs to Bell, Jr., 12 December 1938, Bell Papers.

compelling as fascist aggression. He and Harry Ayers conducted a prolonged debate on the subject, with Ayers defending Churchill's policies toward the Indian subcontinent and Bell pressing for immediate independence.[28]

He was equally prescient regarding China. In 1943 he championed repeal of the nativist Chinese Exclusion Act in order to open America's doors to Chinese displaced by the war. Regarding the postwar future of China, he and his brother speculated that the real struggle would be between communists and Kuomintang after the war with Japan had ended. In both China and India, America should oppose the reimposition of imperialistic and reactionary governments. She should be as thoroughly committed to the establishment of democracy in Asia as she was to winning the war. On this issue he received a sympathetic hearing from Senator Lister Hill:

> I am tremendously interested in what you write me about the situation in the Far East. Vice President Wallace has just left for China. Frankly, I took the liberty of letting him read your letter. I am sure he was as much impressed with what you said as I am. I do not believe that we can build a lasting peace unless we are true to Democracy and its ideals.[29]

Given his international and theological views, it was a short step to pacifism. Bell saw no justification for violence, whether in the realm of domestic labor relations or politics between nations. With restraint and mutual forbearance, statesmen could resolve national differences. During the Second World War, Bell supported Christians who declared themselves conscientious objectors. He corresponded extensively with a young C.O. in Nashville who was sentenced to four years in prison for his beliefs. Bell was actively supportive of the Fellowship of Reconciliation, a national pacifist organization with deep Quaker roots. Brother Tartt worked for the

---

[28]Tartt Bell to Bell, Jr., undated; John H. Bankhead to Bell, Jr., 27 September, 28 October 1942; Harry M. Ayers to Bell, Jr., 18 August, 3 December 1942; Lister Hill to Bell, Jr., 19 October 1942, Bell Papers.

[29]Tartt Bell to Bell, Jr., undated; Lister Hill to Bell, Jr., 22 May 1944, Bell Papers.

fellowship designing strategy and training recruits. Charles Bell contributed financially and helped organize a network of Southern Baptist C.O.'s, which included his friend Clarence Jordan, Dr. Frank Leavell, Charles Maddrey, and others. At the state level, Bell used his influence to lobby for the employment of conscientious objectors at the state mental hospital in Tuscaloosa. Many of the hospital's aides had been drafted, and the use of C.O.'s would fill a critical need. The Selective Service System rejected the proposal, however, bowing to intense pressure from the Veterans of Foreign Wars and the American Legion.[30]

As dear to his heart as was the plight of the nation as it drifted toward war was the position of his own denomination. He watched with horror and incomprehension as Southern Baptists were caught up in the rhetoric of violence. Blind to the domestic and racial injustice within the South, his colleagues seemed only too certain of how to restrain the international violence of a world gone mad. From the big limestone church on Quintard Avenue in Anniston, Bell launched his own offensive for restraint and sanity.

Choosing the most unlikely of settings, Bell proposed his alternative course at the Southern Baptist Convention meeting at New Orleans in May 1937. Each year the Social Service Commission of the S.B.C. presented a resolution on social concerns that was routinely adopted. Commission Director Arthur J. Barton thought of his agency as the conscience of Southern Baptists, but its positions tended to be more a reflection of consensus than prophetic proclamation. The report delivered in New Orleans was no exception. It condemned the use of alcohol, child marriages, large armaments programs, and the use of tobacco by women, preachers, and other church workers. Charlie Bell could hardly believe what he was hearing. When one Oklahoma minister charged that four babies had died in a hospital because their mothers used tobacco, Bell could sit quietly no longer. Addressing the six thousand "messengers," the twenty-eight-year-old minister suggested that perhaps

---

[30]Tartt Bell to Bell, Jr., undated; A. J. Muste to Bell, Jr., 30 April 1943; W. M. Hammond, Jr., to Bell, Jr., 15 December 1942; Dan Whitsett to Bell, Jr., 26 May 1943; Lewis F. Kosch to Bell, Jr., 9 June 1943, Bell Papers.

the children died because their parents could not afford orange juice, fresh vegetables, and nutritious food. Restrained, but very much in earnest, he continued:

> We must face the real issues of life. . . . I cannot adopt such a weak report in a day when we are faced with hunger throughout the land. . . . Why is there nothing in this report condemning conditions among the share-croppers . . .? Starvation wages . . .? You talk about the brotherhood of man. Why, there are Negroes standing outside the door of your convention and you won't let them in! This convention ought to go on record favoring the anti-lynching bill.[31]

Throughout his speech the messengers became increasingly restive, but hearing his plea for racial equality was more than they would tolerate. They greeted his call for support of anti-lynching legislation with shouts of "no, no, no." Georgia's famed "Dry Willie" (William David) Upshaw rose to his feet and announced: "I am going to refute this young man. He is not an old-time Baptist." And with that he launched a vigorous rebuttal. Bell's alternate resolutions addressing the problems of economic and racial injustice drew surprisingly strong support but not enough to pass the convention.

Literally overnight Bell was transformed from an obscure Southern Baptist minister into a controversial denominational leader. Letters poured in from like-minded ministers who had labored in intellectual isolation, despairing at the conservatism and injustice of their communities and at the deadening and irrelevant pietism of their denomination. Suddenly they were aware that, although a distinct minority, there were dozens of them scattered across the South.[32]

Edward A. McDowell, an influential professor at Southern Baptist Seminary, revealed most fully their dilemma in a long, insightful letter to Bell:

---

[31]*Time* (31 May 1937): 57-58; unidentified clipping, Bell Papers.

[32]Charles Dobbins to Bell, Jr., 17 May 1937; Hugh Peterson to Bell, Jr., 5 January 1938, Bell Papers.

> I agree with you that something is wrong in our Southern Baptist life and that something needs to be done. I am thoroughly sympathetic with your views . . . and I wish there were more like you. I hope to do my part here at this strategic place by planting ideas in young preachers' heads.

McDowell suggested that a group of like-minded Southern Baptists should meet the following spring at the Southern Baptist Convention meeting in Richmond to plan a retreat where they could talk about mutual concerns, pray, and enjoy fellowship.

> And this piece of philosophy I pass on to you for what it is worth! I love Southern Baptists—they are *my* people, *my* brethren, and I am going to stay with them unless they run me out. Because I want to stay with them I shall not say all I would like to say all the time, neither will I permit the reactionaries to ''label'' me. I shall engage in controversy as little as possible, and I shall strive always to let *love* be my dominating motive. If people criticize me, I shall love them; if they despise me, I shall love them.[33]

Lonnie W. Meachum, pastor of First Baptist Church in Virginia Beach, Virginia, struggled with similar emotions and contradictions. In 1935, full of idealism and confidence, he boldly preached a sermon on ''The Meaning of Pacifism'' to an uncomprehending congregation. By 1937 he was ''so disgusted by organized religion that sometimes I am almost ready to have done with it.'' His beliefs about war, race, forgiveness, and the brotherhood of man had imperiled his ministry. And worse, his fear for the economic well-being of his wife and three children entrapped him in an awful triangle of family, religious system, and the ethical teachings of Jesus. By 1941 he had despaired. Some members were seeking to fire him and he contemplated leaving the ministry.

Maxie Collins of Batesburg Baptist Church in South Carolina had given up even attending the Southern Baptist Convention:

> It is too bad that even our leaders cannot see the truth or will not. With regard to the race question, economics, and education,

---

[33]Edward A. McDowell, Jr., to Bell, Jr., 4 October 1937, Bell Papers.

not to mention war, I find that while millions of laymen are turning toward the Christian solution, relatively few religious leaders are willing to go all the way with Jesus. Possibly it is too much to expect all men to accept universal brotherhood in reality, but it is not too much to expect them to accept it in principle and do their best to act toward all men as tho all were brothers.

Charlie, what can we do? We have a few souls in S.C. who are laboring—and in every state it is the same. Is it too late to do anything through the church? I am beginning to wonder.[34]

Bell did not share this spirit of pessimism. Such sentiments only provided new urgency to his campaign to change the denomination. After the controversial New Orleans convention, he wrote Arthur Barton, assuring him of his personal respect and support of the Social Service Commission. But he did not waver in his determination to deflect the course of Baptist thought. No sooner had he lost at New Orleans than he was mapping a new strategy for the next convention at Richmond. Two friends at Southern Seminary, W. O. Carver and Harold Tribble, tried to moderate Bell's idealism. Warning him that precipitate action would brand him a radical and destroy his influence, they proposed a gradual campaign. Building on the surprising strength he mustered at New Orleans, he should first contact sympathetic members of the Social Service Commission in hopes of obtaining a favorable report from them. That failing, he should offer a comparatively mild resolution from the floor, holding in reserve an even stronger statement to advance if the messengers seemed favorable to his first proposal. They warned, however, that his confidence in the liberalism of the Richmond area was unfounded. The area was not progressive with respect to race, and the country's "big navy idea" dominated American public opinion.[35]

Bell followed their advice as best he could, pleading with Barton for a more advanced stand on issues. But Barton proved unyield-

---

[34]Lonnie W. Meachum to Bell, Jr., 29 July 1935, 7 April 1937, 21 January 1941; Maxie C. Collins to Bell, Jr., 1 August 1939, Bell Papers.

[35]Arthur J. Barton to Bell, Jr., 2 August 1937; Harold W. Tribble to Bell, Jr., 16 February 1938, Bell Papers.

ing. Bell argued that the commission should be "out in front of our Southern conscience rather than bound by it." Barton reported that step by step the commission had expanded the Baptist conscience on social questions. He even asserted that "our Baptist people have not lagged behind but have really led the Christian bodies of America in taking sane, constructive positions on all social questions." Bell was amazed by what he read, although Barton's contradictory conclusion was nearer the truth:

> You will recognize, of course, that no great serious minded body of Christians will go much if at all beyond their conscience in making united declarations on any question. . . . Those occupying positions of leadership have great responsibility . . . properly to understand and interpret, and to express the conscience and convictions of a great constituency and not to violate this conscience and conviction so as to make their efforts futile.[36]

Tribble acknowledged that Bell had tried to follow proper procedures and despaired of more advanced leadership so long as Barton "does the thinking for the Commission." The only recourse was another challenge to the report at Richmond, with no better results than at New Orleans.[37]

Ever the persuader, Bell sought different avenues of influence. He submitted a lengthy rationale for Christian pacifism to his friend, L. L. Gwaltney, who edited *The Alabama Baptist*. In his own way Gwaltney was as much a mugwump as Bell, having taken numerous controversial stands on evolution, capitalism, and other issues. But he did not share Bell's pacifism and begged him to reconsider the essay. Gwaltney respected too much the right of freedom of speech and press to reject the article, but argued at length against his premises. He dismissed Bell's scriptural references contending that Jesus directed the Sermon on the Mount at his disciples, that pacifism could not be made an ethic for highly organized governments led by non-Christians. In an ideal world,

---

[36]Barton to Bell, Jr., 19 April 1938, Bell Papers.

[37]Harold W. Tribble to Bell, Jr., 25 April 1938, Bell Papers.

such ethical notions might work, but not in the real world of Hitlerism and international lawlessness.

Bell would not relent and Gwaltney was as good as his word. Print it he did and Bell must have been gratified by the response even if Gwaltney was not. Several influential Alabama pastors praised the essay as a "masterful presentation on the Christian attitude toward this entire situation. . . ." John Buchanan, influential pastor of Birmingham's Southside Baptist Church, which was one of the wealthiest and most influential congregations in the state, found himself "more in accord with the spirit and essence of this article than the resolution adopted by the Convention. I think it is unfortunate that the Southern Baptist Convention . . . declared war even before Mr. Roosevelt and the Congress had seen fit to do so." Montague Cook, pastor of Southside Baptist in Montgomery, agreed:

> The position taken by the leaders of the Convention is an unfortunate one. They have left the Master. It is our duty to keep the teachings and method of Christ before the people. In such a way they will see that these who would lead them by the paths of rationalization into murder, are not worthy to be followed.[38]

Alabama friends such as Gwaltney were more willing to humor what they regarded as Bell's eccentricities than were denominational leaders who grew weary of his entreaties. To Bell's request for distribution of material on pacifism at the Southern Baptist Assembly grounds at Ridgecrest, North Carolina, J. L. Lambdin replied that the policy of the Sunday School Board was "to teach genuine Christian citizenship and to do nothing which would be interpreted as being disloyal. . . . With this in mind, it is not wise to have pacifist propaganda at Ridgecrest."

But Bell was indefatigable and repeatedly challenged Baptists to a different position. Even friends who shared some of his convictions warned that the S.B.C. annual convention was controlled by emotion, not reason. When Bell sought to ask the Alabama state

---

[38]L. L. Gwaltney to Bell, Jr., 3 June 1941; John H. Buchanan to Bell, Jr., 13 June 1941; Montague Cook to Bell, Jr., 16 June 1941, Bell Papers.

convention for funds to help conscientious objectors, Buchanan advised that such a request would be fruitless and would only provoke "unwise and unchristian" debate that would harm both the convention and conscientious objectors. Bell admitted that Buchanan was right. Baptist friends in other states concluded that no changes would be made until there were scores of funerals in the denomination.[39] And even that sentiment overestimated the liberalism of the rising generation of Southern Baptist pastors.

More painful perhaps than the rejection of his notion of social justice by right-wing elements within the denomination was the steady deterioration of religious affiliation by left-wing friends. Disillusioned by the church's halfhearted commitment to economic and racial justice, many of Bell's acquaintances drifted out of organized religion. One friend, who finally became a communist, best expressed the disillusion in a long and troubling letter:

> As far as ideals are concerned, Charlie, I have more than I ever had. As far as any mysticism is concerned—I have less than I ever had. I couldn't be completely honest any other way. You speak, too, of me being anti-capital. If there is that in my thinking—it's not on a personal basis. By that, I mean there is no ill-feeling in my heart for any individual, be he capitalist or what not. However, when I see the suffering and the growing decay caused by putting the control of everything into fewer and fewer hands—then my intense desire for the greatest good for the greatest number causes me to honestly and sincerely be opposed to that tendency in our economic system. And I'm more and more convinced that the character of the men involved has very little to do with it. The march of mankind is straining at bonds to break into a more glorious day for everybody, and the favored position of a top few has the objective results of blocking this drive, and as a result thrusting mankind into starvation in the midst of plenty, war, and all the sufferings that follow.
>
> Division there is Charlie—deep basic division. A false sense of smoothing over this division under the guise of promoting unity

---

[39]J. E. Lambdin to Bell, Jr., 10 June 1934; John H. Buchanan to Bell, Jr., 4 February 1942; John W. Inzer to Bell, Jr., 28 April 1942; James H. Ivey to Bell, Jr., undated, Bell Papers.

just prolongs the honest facing of that division, and the clean-cut move to find an answer to it. America needs complete honesty desperately in this hour, but also fearless honesty that will delve right on down and face everything.

I have an abiding faith in the great thousands of ordinary people. But it will take organization and rallying for their honesty and unselfishness to become the dominating thing in American life.[40]

More traumatic even than this was his brother's growing cynicism toward the church. Charles and Tartt had always been close, with the older brother an obvious source of intellectual and spiritual inspiration to the younger. While a student at Tulane, Tartt was still quite obviously under his brother's spell, idealistic and attracted to Kagawa, Gerald Nye, and the Fellowship of Reconciliation. But as the depression deepened and war became a reality, Tartt drifted farther from his brother's world. During his work for a Master's degree in economics at the University of Chicago, Tartt largely ignored his chosen field to probe new intellectual depths which he had missed at Tulane. Andre Malraux, Dostoyevsky, John Steinbeck, Thorstein Veblen, Frederick Engles, John Dos Passos, and Clifford Odets jarred him with new visions of the world. His previous reading had been "very puritanical," but his remedial education called old values into question. He was disappointed in Franklin Roosevelt for remaining in the reactionary Democratic party. If only FDR would forge labor and the left into a new party it would be "a glorious start for a real progressive group." And he inquired politically of his brother: "Still content to call yourself a liberal and cooperate with anybody that comes along, or are you developing some more definite ideas about what you want and how to get it?"[41] Suspended between the values of his family and their religion and the new secular values emerging within the disillusioned intellectual community, Tartt challenged his older brother's conscience.

***

[40]S. J. to Bell, Jr., 5 August 1940, Bell Papers.

[41]Three letters from Tartt Bell to Bell, Jr., all undated but between 1936-1942, Bell Papers.

A Christmas reunion in the early war years provided the setting for a painful confrontation. Upon his return to Chicago, Tartt admitted how difficult it was to talk to his elder brother anymore. He felt intellectually out of place in Anniston, no longer sharing the same ideas, habits, and appetites which they once had in common. Recognizing his older brother's commitment to the social gospel, he could not comprehend Charlie's inaction in the face of so wicked a world. While sharing a meal with his brother's enlightened Anniston friends, Tartt could only think:

> Here sit a group of around 50 people, wonderfully well meaning in their desires to uplift themselves and others, individually well-adjusted to society, who have the dynamic for a revolution right here in the city. And further, they are all doing something about it. And yet they are losing a marvelous chance to make their efforts and hopes effective because they don't see beyond this concern with individual problems.
>
> My goodness. Charlie, if people like yourself who certainly mean well aren't going to do anything about it, what is to be expected?
>
> You have a leader and speaker, yourself. You have access to the press, Charles Dobbins. You have finances. You have freedom and courage. Why if a communist group had half what you have there they would be virtually running the town. I see no reason why, with a little political strategy, even if it means mass meetings, leaflets, anything at all, you couldn't put over some real reforms there in Anniston. And this very group—any church group for that matter—offers a great opportunity. Further it *should* be leading the revolution, both social and individual.[42]

What Tartt could not know in his youthful exuberance was how high the price of revolution in Anniston was and how painful were the wounds. Charlie knew only too well. The storms that he had loosed within the Southern Baptist Convention had left him largely unscathed, but the controversies he stirred in Parker Memorial cost him dearly.

---

[42]Ibid., sometime in the early 1940s.

As early as 1937 Bell vowed to leave Anniston. Seminary friends found a more congenial church in Paducah, Kentucky, but members of that congregation found out about the controversial Oxford Group and sought Bell's pledge not to institute such activities in the Kentucky parish. This he would not give them and the negotiations ended. At this critical juncture his old professor, W. O. Carver, warned him of the factionalism he was creating at Parker. Carver believed that Bell could become one of the most significant and prophetic leaders of the denomination, but he must exercise caution and restraint: "You can easily become a thwarted martyr to an ideal, instead of a compelling witness to and exponent of an idea—even of the Christ who incarnates the ideal."[43]

Caught between the extravagant expectations of his friends and brother and the pragmatic strategy of advisers such as Carver, Bell struggled to express his own convictions. In 1938 he resigned his pastorate at Parker Memorial. The occasion was an agonizing compromise he had made with the deacons regarding the Oxford Group. So divisive had the little fellowship become that he agreed to stop its meetings for two years in order to allow the church to put aside its internal strife. As logical as the agreement was for the sake of harmony, it so rankled his conscience and compromised him morally that he finally returned to the deacons to offer his resignation. But for the powerful position of his father and the active support of Harry Ayers, that would have ended his association with the church. However, a deacon employed at his father's bank caught the other deacons quite by surprise by proposing that if Bell felt compromised by his pledge regarding the Oxford Group, the church should relieve him of the obligation to honor the pledge. The resolution passed on a standing vote that some in the church interpreted as a strategy to keep Bell. Many members cared so much for Bell's parents that they could not bring themselves to publicly oppose their son.[44]

---

[43]Edward A. McDowell, Jr., to Bell, Jr., 27 September 1937; George D. Heaton to Bell, Jr., 17 November 1937; W. O. Carver to Bell, Jr., 9 September 1937, Bell Papers.

[44]Oral history with Charles R. Bell, Jr.

Local ministers and friends congratulated him on the support of his congregation, but one of his New York mentors in the Oxford Movement wrote more bluntly. Many of Bell's problems stemmed not from his adherence to the philosophy of the Oxford Movement but from his own impetuousness. Fundamentally Bell was an individualist and an isolationist who neither sought advice nor sustained a disciplined commitment to the Oxford ideas:

> I feel your tendency, Charlie, is to want to check something after it has reached a crisis instead of checking the policy which could have prevented the crisis. . . . It is not a question of courage or cowardice; it is a question of guided strategy thoroughly checked versus impulsive or routine or otherwise unguided courses of action. As things are, it seems to me you made people take up an attitude toward the Oxford Group which they do not understand and of which they have had no adequate demonstration. Of course, trouble results.
>
> . . . There is entirely too much laying down of conditions and entirely too little living of a life, if you ask my opinion, Charlie.[45]

Paradoxically Bell's younger brother advised a directly contradictory course. Disappointed that his elder brother had consented to the two-year moratorium in the first place, he advised "do absolutely what you feel that you should do with no compromises"; "to heck with what anybody else thinks; I hope you do what you will be absolutely satisfied with."[46]

In the end that is just what Charles Bell did. The issue that ended his pastorate at Parker Memorial seems almost anticlimactic after the clashes on so many issues. Church members were determined to hang a plaque honoring Parker's members who served in the military and display a flag in honor of the righteousness of the nation's cause. Although Bell felt any national flag within the church identified Christ too much with an attitude of national exclusiveness, the flag itself was not the primary issue; the timing of the event primarily troubled him. By displaying the flag after Amer-

---

[45]"Sam" to Bell, Jr., 10 October 1939, Bell Papers.

[46]Tartt Bell to Bell, Jr., undated, Bell Papers.

ica declared war, it became a symbol of armed might. Despite Bell's objections, the deacons commissioned a U.S. service flag with stars placed in the form of a cross. All other churches in the community had such flags and they were determined that Parker would also.

Aware of their plans, Bell sought the advice of friends and family, who responded with ingenious if somewhat devious stratagems. One proposed to let soldiers in the congregation vote on whether they sought such symbolism in the church. With large numbers training for overseas duty at nearby Fort McClellan, he felt they had more important concerns on their minds. Others urged him to state frankly his own views but to abide by the majority decision of his congregation. By so doing he might educate them, if they did not dismiss him as pastor. Finally even Tartt understood the gravity of the situation and advised moderation. Bell should once again state his objections as fairly as possible, granting that some sincerely believed in a different course. He should not start with an ultimatum that if they displayed the flag, he would resign. His brother Alex offered similar advice, adding that Bell need not worry about the fate of wife Ann or son Charles III. He would provide financial support so long as they needed it.

Thus fortified, Bell faced his final battle at Parker. To identify the church with war simply because all the other congregations in Anniston were doing so was clearly unchristian. The crisis would come when they asked him to participate in the ceremony to hang the flag. And this he would not do.[47]

Bell was able to delay the final confrontation until D-Day in June 1944. But as news of the European invasion blared from radios throughout town, members trekked to the church determined to have their flag displayed regardless of their pastor's scruples. Nor could Bell back down on an issue, which for him was central to all religious values.

Some of his antagonists evidenced no spirit of Christian love, demonstrating perhaps how right Bell was, how much the war had

---

[47]"Jim" to Bell, Jr., 1 February 1944; Ralph T. Templin to Bell, Jr., 12 October 1942; Tartt Bell to Bell, Jr., 8 November 1942; Alex Bell to Bell, Jr., undated; Bell, Jr., to "Jim," undated, Bell Papers.

dried up the wellsprings of love and good will. One anonymous parishioner wrote his pastor, carefully noting that a carbon copy also had been sent to Bell's father:

> I want to congratulate you on your resignation. That is the best thing you have done for our church in ten or more years. Stick to your resignation. Don't let the two-faced ones in the congregation vote you back.
>
> In your first resignation many voted to retain you because it was a standing vote and they did not wish to hurt your father and mother by voting against you. If it had been by secret ballot the only ones who would have voted to retain you would have been those crack-brained Oxford Movementites [*sic*].
>
> The people are tired of a negro loving traitor to our flag. . . . The place for you is in a negro church in Harlem or Springfield, Missouri.
>
> The congregation is sorry for your mother and father, but they have no sympathy for you and your yellow to the core brothers. . . . A white person who believes in social equality is lower than the lowest negro alive. . . . A very potential danger to our South will be removed when you shake the dust of Alabama from your feet.[48]

Iva Cook, society editor of the *Anniston Star* and a longtime family friend, tried to be more reconciling. If ever he got "straightened out on your war attitude and the Negro question I am ready to throw my arms around you and fight for you."[49] From far and wide friends communicated their support. Fellow Baptists within the state and across the convention praised his courage. One of them expressed the prevailing opinion: "Thank God for you and men like you!" Word spread quickly and ministers of other denominations sent letters of support.

But perhaps the letters that meant most to Anniston's Pilgrim, sunk into his own "slough of despond," came from his parishioners. His efforts had not been entirely in vain, for laymen who could not leave Anniston risked much to defend him. In their letters

---

[48]"A Member" to Bell, Jr., 13 June 1944, Bell Papers.

[49]Iva Cook to Bell, Jr., undated, Bell Papers.

they testified to his influence and their own spiritual maturity acquired through his guidance. One letter from an Annistonian put the entire matter in simple biblical perspective: "Jesus said, 'Darkness hateth the light because their deeds are evil.' In other words, when men's desires are to murder their fellow man contrary to God's law which reads 'Thou shalt not kill' naturally they want to find fault with those who teach the truth."[50]

Bell did not wait long to begin anew. The Fellowship of Reconciliation tendered him a position, but he declined, desiring to stay in the pulpit. On Bell's behalf, his old friend, John Buchanan, contacted Dr. Edwin McNeill Poteat, who then was teaching at Rochester Colgate Seminary. Buchanan believed Bell would be better accepted among Northern Baptists. Poteat bemoaned how churches "cut off their own noses to spite their faces," but could offer little encouragement: "Unfortunately the North is no more tolerant of men of his opinions than the South. . . . On the war issue, North and South are unanimous, and though the South may appear more volatile and ready to act more quickly, the North's moderation is nonetheless quite as resolute and decisive."[51]

On this score, Poteat was wrong. He wrote to the Rev. L. B. Moseley, a friend who was about to leave the pastorate of First Baptist Church, Madison, Wisconsin, recommending the Alabama pastor. Moseley had followed Bell's career from his dramatic presentation at the S.B.C. meeting in New Orleans through his prophetic essay on race in the *Christian Century*, and assured him that the issues that had so divided Parker would not disturb the Madison congregation:

> In twelve years this church has supported me in preserving a free pulpit. I have never had any church that responded to the po-

---

[50]For samples of reactions, see S. J. Ezell to Bell, Jr., 30 June 1944; "Jim" to Bell, Jr., 10 July 1944; H. Ross Arnold to Bell, Jr., 30 June 1944; Dr. T. W. Ayers to Bell, Jr., 4 October 1944; Sam Eby to Bell, Jr., 2 August 1944. For reactions from within Parker, see especially John L. Cottrell to Bell, Jr., 19 June 1944; Alex and Nan Hall to Bell, Jr., 21 June 1944; W. B. Crabb to Bell, Jr., 15 June 1944, Bell Papers.

[51]John H. Buchanan to Edwin McNeill Poteat, 3 July 1944; Poteat to Buchanan, 12 July 1944, Bell Papers.

sition of Jesus as I think this church has responded. Matters which trouble you in Alabama will be taken for granted here, unless you do too much about them. You understand that the Kingdom of God will not come without opposition. But this town listens and responds.

   . . . You can be a prophet and stay in Madison.

Moseley knew whereof he spoke, for his own spiritual pilgrimage had paralleled Bell's. A native of Selma, Alabama, he had attended Baptist Wake Forest University in North Carolina and Southern Baptist Theological Seminary before accepting a Northern Baptist pastorate. Numbered among his congregation were three blacks, two Japanese Americans, many Southerners, and scattered peoples from around the world.[52]

Bell enjoyed a successful and satisfying tenure in Madison before ending his career as pastor of First Baptist Church, Pasadena, California, and retiring to Arizona. Although he mellowed a bit, especially on strategy and method, his basic convictions remained constant. Forged as they were in the cauldron of Anniston's religious fires, they were hard as steel.

Sitting on the front porch of Bell's family home in Anniston on a lazy summer day in 1972, two former parishioners of Parker Memorial Baptist Church reflected upon their separate spiritual pilgrimages. We had both changed, but my change had been the painless sort wrought by perceptive teachers at the Baptist college we shared in common and by the ethical liberalism of the 1960s. In many ways we sought the same kind of world and shared a common Christian ideology. But my commitment had cost little; in a perverse kind of way it was even fashionable. He had been mostly out of joint with his times and carried the scar tissue to prove it. Bell, eyes still afire with energy, recounted his dream of rural cooperatives. As he warmed to the subject, his voice became more animated. He leaned forward in his rocking chair and his hands gestured vigorously:

---

[52]L. B. Moseley to Bell, Jr., 6 August 1944, Bell Papers.

I feel that the American economy has simply got to come to some kind of principle where there is a fair division of our wealth. I mean I think all these social problems we are working on—it's foolish to continue hoping that we are going to resolve them until we resolve a more equitable distribution of our income. . . . You can't expect to have any kind of social justice with a man like Aristotle Onassis owning a thousand million dollars and some Negro boy here in Anniston not able to get an education. I mean revolution is going to come out of that. No way for any kind of social justice to be equated with that.[53]

---

[53]Oral history with Charles R. Bell, Jr.

Index

MP *Clearings in the Thicket*

Designed by: Margaret Jordan Brown
Composition by MUP Composition Department
Production specifications:
  text paper—60 pound Warren's Olde Style
  endpapers—Multicolor Antique Cafe
  cover—(on .088 boards) Holliston Roxite Crown Linen 13460
  dust jacket—100 pound enamel. Printed three colors PMS 355 (green),
  PMS 467 (tan), and Black. Varnished.

Printing (offset lithography) and binding by Omnipress of Macon, Inc.,
  Macon, Georgia